Aloha . . . Forever

Aloha...Forever

by

Mark and Diane Yasuhara

Harrison, Arkansas

Unless otherwise noted all biblical quotations are taken from the New American Standard Bible, copyright by the Lockman Foundation, LaHabra, California.

©1975 by New Leaf Press. All rights reserved. Published by New Leaf Press, Harrison, Arkansas 72601.

Printed in United States of America

Library of Congress Card Number: 75-21285

ISBN 0-89221-007-9

Contents

1	Beginning	7
2	Childhood	15
3	Teen Years	27
4	College Days	37
5	Little Brown Gal Meets Funny Little Guy	50
6	Together	56
7	A Few Years Older Than Our Son	63
8	Our Son Fred	74
9	Waiting, Waiting	89
10	Mainland Ministry	105
11	Ruby	111
12	The Beginning of Something Big	118
13	On Our Way	128
14	Aloha . . . the Forever Kind	133

1
Beginning

As a child, my father, who was being raised as a Buddhist, was covered with hives. He was screaming and carrying on because the pain was unbearable. As was the custom of Buddhists, his mother took him to the temple. The priest took my father, who was in his early elementary years, picked him up, and held him straight out in front of him. He gargled some *sake* (Japanese rice wine) in his mouth and spit it all over my father and his hives left immediately! This wasn't any mickey mouse stuff; they had faith in their gods and it worked.

My mother is a real Hawaiian, but she doesn't look like the typical Hawaiian. She's very fair and she doesn't have the big nose characteristic of most Hawaiians.

My dear ancestors come from way, way, way back. They surely were on the beach when Captain Cook's ship sailed into the bay. They were the indigenous Hawaiians—people who migrated all the way from the South Sea islands of Polynesia to Hawaii a couple of thousand years ago. They settled there and developed their own culture.

My mother's parents were converted to Catholicism,

for most of the Hawaiians had been converted to some kind of "Christian" religion by the early 1900s—so today they're either Catholics, Mormons, or Protestants.

My mom and dad went to the same high school, and my mother was very good friends with the Yasuhara boys.

Mrs. Procter was just a young lady when God called her to Hawaii from Atlanta, Georgia. She didn't know beans about the place. All she knew was that God called her to the Hawaiian Islands. She came over all by herself and settled in the city of Hilo. Soon she set up an afternoon storytime for the neighborhood children. My parents, as kids, were running around and they stopped in on her storytime. It wasn't long until they accepted Jesus. Just think, Mrs. Procter had come all the way from Atlanta to settle in the neighborhood so my parents could know the Lord. They really got turned on to Jesus.

One day Mrs. Procter took a group of the oldest and most spiritually mature kids down to the beach for a special prayer meeting. The next day in school these kids were just glowing. My mom, dad, and their friends asked, "What's happened to you?"

They said, "Oh, it's so wonderful. It's so wonderful. Jesus is so real!"

Eventually Anna and Albert, my mother and father, got to go down to the beach. They were told about the Holy Spirit and His power, and there on the beach Jesus inundated them with a tidal wave of His Holy Spirit. They used to pray there with all the waves dashing against the rocks in the light of the big Hawaiian moon. (The "moon of Manakura" never saw the likes of this!) Many times they'd stay until about four o'clock in the morning and just pray in the Spirit.

By the time my parents were in their teens, both of

their mothers had become Christians. My grandfathers never took much interest in the things of the Lord. For some reason, Hawaiian men are not really open to the gospel. I think it has a lot to do with the corruption of the gospel message the early missionaries brought over. If you read the book or saw the movie *Hawaii* by James Michener, you'd realize that he didn't give the missionaries very good treatment. They were sincere people initially, but many of them were sidetracked and became hoodlums in the whole rape of Hawaii.

But that isn't altogether the whole truth. Without the missionaries, we would never have known Jesus. But one of the most tragic things which happened was the Westernization of all the converts. It's not that we minded having to wear clothes, but, for example, my mother and father, being part of a fundamental church, were taught that things like the hula were part of a heathen culture and were worldly and evil.

It seemed that all the missionaries from the mainland were ultra-super-conservative, and that their Christianity demanded a conformation to Western culture.

When I was in junior high school, one of these new ministers, who had come from the mainland, stood up in our denomination's district council and said that he didn't think we should have mixed bathing. I remember my father saying that he at first agreed. But what he didn't know then—he found out later—was that the conscientious minister meant plain old swimming! Now can you imagine coming to Hawaii and telling these people that they shouldn't be swimming together? My uncle, who was the assistant district superintendent, got up and said, "Look, there was a time when we used to swim together naked. So you better be glad that we at least have clothes on now." The new missionary sat down and didn't say anymore.

But there were many things imposed upon the people of Hawaii. The missionaries brought their culture with them and because they knew their religion was superior, they thought everything about them was superior. The men of Hawaii saw through this and turned the missionaries off. I don't know of many Hawaiian men, from indigenous Hawaiian ancestry, who really have made a stand for Christ.

The Caucasian-Christian superiority-separation was most evident in the early educational system. My brother and I went to Hilo Union School. (There are four children in the family. My brother, Albert Matthew, is one year older than I. My younger brother is Woodrow Luke, and the fourth child is Amy Ann. So there's Matthew, Mark, Luke, and Amy Ann, but she likes to call herself Amy John!)

My father was an assistant pastor under Rev. Peter Funk and his wife. Their son was the same age as my brother, so they started elementary school at the same time, except that the Funk's son went to the Riverside Elementary School across the street. Riverside Elementary was started by the Caucasian people; they called it the English Standard School because all the local kids talked a lot of pidgin English, and they didn't want their children to be corrupted with that kind of language.

My parents knew it wasn't only because of the language that they didn't want them to be mixed, but many of the *haole* parents didn't want their kids socializing with the local kids. Everybody knew that; it was just accepted. We didn't feel bitter or resentful about it except that my father said, "You will go to Hilo Union School and you will be just as good as all those *haole* kids going to Riverside."

Well, as a matter of fact, the year after my sixth grade

graduation from Hilo Union, Riverside became Hilo Union Annex. That was like a minor victory for my parents, for they had also gone to Hilo Union. All the children of the plantation owners and children of the missionaries went to Riverside, but now it's a special education school for all the slow kids. That is a switch!

About dancing the hula. Hula is a beautiful art form which was sacred to the old Hawaiians. A large portion of the ancient hulas were written to honor the monarchy. But when the missionaries came, some of them wanted to do away with all this. These missionaries taught a strict fundamentalism which excluded dancing. So hula was out! My mother always wanted to learn to do the hula, but she felt that it would be a stumbling block to people. But she secretly thought it was okay.

So Diane and I do the hula now. We could still be Hawaiian and give sacred concerts and not do the hula, but we do it because we think we should. I don't want anyone to think that because we are Christians we don't dance the hula, and I don't want anyone to think that because we are Christians we are not supposed to dance the hula. It's an integral part of my Hawaiian culture, my Hawaiian heritage, and I think it's a part that should be preserved and perpetuated.

(I like to tell people that if they think the hula is very wicked, the hula which people do here on the mainland is very wicked too. After all, the hula is only a Polynesian "Deep and Wide"!)

My father started working for the S. H. Kress Company as a stock boy when he was fourteen. Just after my brother and I were born, my parents (I guess they were in their early twenties) were encouraged by the pastor to go to the mainland and attend the Eastern Bible Institute in Pennsylvania, for a year of study. My father and mother really wanted to serve the Lord, so my father left his job, seniority and all. They traveled around and itinerated with the pastor and his wife. It was a great experience for a young Hawaiian couple straight from the "bushes." However, it really affected their concept of "living by faith."

My father told me, when I was growing up and thinking of going into the ministry, "Mark, that's all fine and good, but at least learn a trade." That's all he would say.

But my mother was a little more candid; she always was. She'd say, "Yes, it's all right to live by faith if you can go back to the mainland and itinerate every seven years and get your offerings coming in. You know, it's okay for people from the mainland to live on faith because they have people supporting them. But who's going to support you? Because the people here in Hawaii can't support you, and you're not going to be able to go to the mainland and get any support."

So I was raised with this kind of "dented" sense of faith. Trust in God, but learn a trade—just in case!

The whole thing about the missionary was really trusting what the missionary said and lived. All we knew about God was how the missionary interpreted the Bible. It occurred to me about four or five years ago that the only thing I knew about God was what I was told about Him—the interpretation I had been given by somebody else. As someone said, "The only spiritual food a lot people get is what the minister digested himself and then regurgitated on the Sunday morning congregation."

So my parents went back to Hawaii a little wiser. My father went back to the S. H. Kress company and although he had lost all of his seniority, he's finally worked to being manager. His store has become one of the top ten Kress stores in the nation.

My mother finally got her R.P.N. degree last year. So now she's qualified to nurse and care for old people. She takes care of her family during the day and then goes to the nursing home at ten or eleven o'clock at night and stays there until six in the morning. She then comes back and takes care of her own home. She has more energy than a lot of people half her age.

During my senior year in high school, I found out that one of the boys who was coming to church was living up in the attic of the church—hiding out from his mother. I invited Wilson to hide in our basement; it was three days before my folks found out. I begged my parents to please let him live with us because he needed a home. So he became my parents' first foster child.

To this day they have had over thirty foster children and most of them have stayed from four to seven years. Because of the limited space, their home does not meet the qualifications for a welfare foster home, so only when the social services don't have anywhere else to place a child, they take him to my parents. Now most of the older kids have grown up to become beautiful Christians and they call my mother and father "mom and dad."

The younger children are hard for them to give up. They told the social worker, "No babies, because it breaks our hearts when the baby is adopted out a year later. Give us a baby that no one wants and that no one will ever want. Give us your sickest, ugliest, worst-looking child." Sure enough, the social service called one day and said, "We have a baby like you described. No one will ever take this child."

Quinton was four months old and he looked like he was two weeks old. He was blue and discolored and he never cried; he just whimpered softly. One side of his head was flat because he had laid on that side all the time since he was born. He had had pneumonia and all kinds of sicknesses. But in about two months he was the healthiest, most robust baby around. (Of course, you know those old-time Pentecostals had prayed for him, too!) When he was about four years old someone adopted him. My parents still cry today when they think of precious little Quinton.

So from childhood I saw real, tangible love extended to others and that was in time going to change the course of my life.

2
Childhood

I was three years old when I sang my first solo. That was in Allentown, Pennsylvania, for a Christmas program. My brother and I were supposed to sing together but he chickened out, so I told my father, "I will, Daddy, I will!" That was just an indication of things to come.

My father has always called me a grandstander. I went up there then and sang a solo, complete with hand motions. I didn't know a three-year-old should hardly be able to carry a melody, much less do the motions with it, but I guess I was what you'd call gifted. I didn't know it. I guess nobody knew it.

When I was five years old, my favorite song was "Follow, I Will Follow Thee." Every time we'd sing this song in church I would cry. I remember telling the other kids in kindergarten, "I'll sing a song for you if you like," and then I'd sail into the chorus of "Follow, I will Follow Thee". I never understood why they always ran off laughing, as though I were some kind of nut.

I could harmonize when I was in kindergarten, and by the time I was in first grade I could read the alto part in the hymnal along with my mother. Again, none of us thought that was anything special.

When I was in kindergarten, I had a dream that all the members of my family were cut-out hearts laying on the closet floor (like flannelgraph hearts in Sunday school: black hearts, red hearts, and white hearts). We were all black hearts. Then everybody came to Jesus but me. I could see His blood cover their hearts. Then my father, my mother, and my older brother became white hearts because they accepted Jesus. But I was still a black heart. Jesus lived on the top shelf of the closet—the top shelf was where my mother kept all the things she didn't want me to touch. So it was like heaven and Jesus was up there.

One day Jesus came back, reached out His hand and all the white hearts flew up to the top shelf. But I was a black heart, so I was left behind. I tried so hard to reach the top shelf. I can remember my mother reaching down and trying, trying to reach . . . I had this image of one hand reaching up and one hand reaching down. All I could do was scream, "Mommy! Mommy!"

I saw that scene again in Michelangelo's "The Creation of Adam" in the Sistine Chapel and exclaimed, "That's just like my dream!" That dream was my first recollection of having the need of a Savior.

In our church they had altar calls every time they had a service. So at each service I went down to make sure I was born again . . . again . . . and again.

Every night my brother and I would pray, "God bless mommy and daddy, gramma and grampa. Keep us safe, and help us not to have bad dreams."

As a child I had nightmares all the time. Take one of the dreams I had. It was Halloween and the church had had a big social down in the basement. My mother said, "Now, Mark, whatever you do, do not go out into the street and play." Well, a bunch of us went out and we trick-or-treated up and down the block and did a lot of funny stuff. Nobody found out. Then I came downstairs to the social and all I saw was a huge platter of glazed donuts. But when I went over to the donuts and reached out for one of them, a lady put a cloth over them and said, "Oh, I'm sorry, the social's all over." And I woke up crying.

To this day, when I see glazed donuts, I just can't get enough of them.

When I was nine, an evangelist came to the church to preach on the latter days and the antichrist; I'd come home terrified. I had nightmares every night and they were continuations of the same thing—in one dream the communists had come and locked up my mother and father in my grandfather's pigpen.

One night I was too afraid to go to sleep. I wasn't going to go to sleep until I was absolutely sure that if the Lord came I was going to go to heaven. I was too embarrassed to talk with my father and mother, so I went into the bathroon.

My parents were very active in the church and both of them had to work, so we hardly had any time together. We didn't go on a vacation at all until I was in junior high school. We didn't have holidays, and the only time we went on picnics was with the church.

I rarely confided in my mother and father. In fact, I don't remember my mother or father saying to me, when I was a child, "I love you," or holding me, or saying, "I'm sorry." That's important to me now, because it means a lot, My folks never kissed me, never hugged me. Its not that they didn't love me; they just weren't into heavy "huggy and kissy" about it. So I didn't want to talk to my parents about my fears. I was afraid, I guess.

I locked myself in the bathroom and made believe I had diarrhea. I stayed in there for I don't know how long; it seemed like the longest time. I cried and cried to Jesus, "Jesus, don't let me go to sleep. I'm not going to go to sleep until I'm absolutely sure that I'll go to heaven."

The assurance came when I got tired of sitting on the toilet! I kept saying, "God, You've got to do it! You've got to do it!" I think that's really where it was at for me because the Lord had already taken care of it. He just saw this as being silly. So He said, "Well, you can just sit there as long as you want."

Finally I went to bed and the Lord instilled the peace in my heart while I was sleeping. It wasn't a big thing, but it was what I needed to know. I knew this peace was mine because I had no more bad dreams and have never doubted my salvation from that day to this!

It wasn't so much that I wanted to know if I would go to heaven—I just didn't want to have any more bad dreams! But I guess that was a good sign.

A little walkway came in from the road to the three houses on the lane where I lived. Each of the houses had about two acres of land around it, overgrown with huge trees and jungle bushes. It was a paradise for us kids. Our house was the middle house, and the houses on either side had gone into disrepair so they had been condemned. We had the entire place to ourselves.

The person who had lived in the house before we did was a *kahuna* lady—she was like a witchdoctor. Even though Christianity had come to the islands, many of the people who knew *kahuna* still practiced it. The Hawaiians knew who was who. They knew who had it and who didn't. I don't know how my mother knew, but being Hawaiian, she knew this lady was a *kahuna* lady.

At first, my parents wouldn't let us go down into the basement and play. It was there that the *kahuna* lady had practiced her witchcraft. They went down there to clean the whole thing out. I don't know what all was down there, but there were lots of rings, trinkets, cloths, pictures, and other things that my parents took out and burned. It was too bad because a lot of the things were old Hawaiian artifacts. We weren't to have any of that in the house because it was evil. I guess it was, but I was sorry they had to burn it all.

During the first couple of weeks we lived in the house, my mother had the strangest thing happen to her. My father was either at church or at work, and at night she would hear someone calling her, "Annaaaaa . . . Annaaaaa."

She would go outside to the front porch and say, "Yes, yes, who is it?" But nobody was there.

She'd go back into the house and again she would hear, "Annaaaa . . . Annaaaaa."

Again she'd go out and nobody would be there. My mother started feeling spooky, So when it happened the third time, she screamed at the top of her voice, "In Jesus' name, I take dominion over you, Satan, and I cast you out of this place!"

The voices never came back. But then my mother really had a scream—and she knew what to scream.

But for several weeks we would hear this *rhrrrrrrrrdtdtdtdtdt . . . rhrrrrrrrrrrdtdtdtdtdtdt* up in our attic while we tried to sleep. This would never happen until everything was very quiet late at night. The people who lived in the house before we did were there only a couple of months because they said it was haunted. Now we knew why we got it so cheaply. We were renting a haunted house!

My father, being the wise father that he was, soon

calmed our fears. We had a large macadamia nut tree in the back of the house; the macadamia nut is a small, round, hard nut. The rats would take the nuts and roll them across the floor of the attic and then run after them. My father put rat poison up there and that was the end of those demons!

It was too bad that my parents rarely let us out of the yard. As far as we knew, none of our friends anywhere around there were Christians and my father didn't want us to play at the homes of non-Christians. So they would come over to our house to play.

I remember when I was in the sixth grade and my father was home on vacation. One of my pals let out a long string of cuss words. My father simply turned to him and said, "Look, if you're going to talk like that, we don't want you to come into our yard." So Gary, Benjie, and all the rest never came back. That's one of the reasons I never had an opportunity to really learn to play baseball.

We lived right next door to the park, but I never could go there and play. They had programs during the summer, but my parents didn't let me attend them. I remember coming home in second grade wanting to join Cub Scouts and being told I couldn't join because Cub Scouts went to the movies. So I didn't have a chance to learn a lot of things other kids learn from playing and from sports. This was really too bad because I had an inferiority complex by the time I was in first grade.

Nobody really knows what it feels like to be left out and rejected until he has two team captains on the ball field fighting over him because neither of them wants him.

First of all, I thought they were all heathens and were all going to hell. And secondly, I couldn't play ball as well as they played. The rest of the kids were really aggressive. Island kids are like that. They are very outdoorsy and athletic. That's why a lot of mainland kids, when they come to Hawaii, get bullied around because the island kids are so physical in their playing and working.

On the other hand, they're not aggressive when it comes to verbalizing. The mainland kids can talk a blue streak and the island kids just sit there and don't say a word. By the time I was halfway through elementary school I had developed such a terrible inferiority complex that I didn't know how to relate with the kids in school. Of course, when my father let loose like that with those neighborhood kids, and they never came back, I had to play by myself.

In spite of that, I was a creative, out-going kid. A child in Hawaii never initiated anything—it was the old "speak when you're spoken to" routine. Somehow I never fit into that. I liked to talk—I guess people would say I was precocious. But I think to my folks and the rest of the adults, I was just a smart-alecky little brat! Only the Lord could have known that I was going to one day be using my "gift of gab" for Him across the mainland.

When I was about seven, my teacher said that the place in the middle of your head is a cowlick, where your hair sticks out and won't lie down. My father had told me it was a giddy-giddy. So I went home and said, "Daddy, my teacher said that's a cowlick."

"Naw," he said, "that's a giddy-giddy." And he just laughed and laughed.

The next day, right in the middle of whatever we were studying, I raised my hand and said, "Miss Hashimoto, can I say something?"

She looked at me—nobody ever interrupts like that—and said, "Well, what is it, Edward?" (I was always called Edward in school.)

I got up and said, "My father said that that's not a cowlick, it's a giddy-giddy."

All the children looked at me and started to giggle. Miss Hashimoto sputtered and said, "Well, you may sit down." I knew I had said something to upset her, but I didn't know what.

Another time we were making presents for our parents during craft time. We were going to make hot-pads for our mothers, dolls for our baby sisters and brothers, and ashtrays for our fathers. Hawaii doesn't have a fundamentalist tradition, but they should have known that some fathers don't smoke. I went home and asked my daddy for a tuna can.

"What do you want a tuna can for, anyway?" he asked.

"I just need it for school," was my reply.

"Well, what for?" he asked again.

"I can't tell you,"

"Well, if you can't tell me, I'm not going to give you a tuna can," he said.

"Daddy, please," I begged. "I've got to have a tuna can real bad."

Well, I had to tell my dad what it was for, and he told me to tell the teacher that he was a Christian and didn't smoke. (My dad wanted me to be a good witness, even in the first grade.) The next day the teacher asked all of us if we had brought our tuna cans. So like a brave little Indian I raised my hand and said, "Mrs. Goo, my father said to tell you that he's a Christian and he doesn't smoke, so he doesn't need an ashtray."

All the kids were aghast. And of course Mrs. Goo had never heard anything so impertinent in her life. So while

I stood there she said, "Children, look at him. Look at him. His father doesn't smoke so he can't bring a tuna can. Now did you ever hear of anything so ridiculous in your whole life?"

They laughed and giggled at me. I couldn't understand why I had to suffer so much.

Because we couldn't go out of the yard, we were constantly making up things to do. Take one year, after TV came out, and I was in the fourth grade. I decided we were going to do a whole series of "cowboys and Indians" shows in our own back yard. I had a little wagon which we were going to build into a covered wagon. I took my kid brother, who was six, and my little sister, who was two, and had them play the part of the early American pioneers.

One day I decided that the Indians would come and set the covered wagon on fire. My father had three prized banana trees at the lower part of our yard—our yard sloped downward. The house was on the upper side of the slope and a walkway went through the middle of the yard. It was at the bottom of the yard where all the bushes started. My father liked to garden whenever he had time, but these three banana trees were his pride and joy.

We kids were going to have the largest Indian attack of all time; we would set fire to the covered wagon and the whole attack would be real, "just like on TV."

The covered wagon was the main prop and would give us the realism and live action that was needed. I took my mother's good store-bought paper window shades and covered the wagon. No makeshift bamboo was going to be used in this wagon.

So I put my brother and sister in the wagon with the proper instructions: "When I push the wagon down the slope, I will set it on fire. You scream and yell real loud like you're dying. When it gets halfway down the slope, you guys jump out, okay?"

"Okay," they said somewhat dubiously.

I lit the fire, pushed the wagon, and down the slope the blazing death trap screamed. I didn't realize how fast the paper shades would burn—I got scared and screamed, "Jump out, jump out! Oh, Jesus, help them jump!"

Just before the fire collapsed into the wagon, the "pioneers" jumped to safety with only skinned knees and bruises. But the wagon kept on careening down the slope—right into my father's prize banana tree! Banana trees have huge dry leaves hanging down and as the wagon hit the tree—*whoosh!*—in seconds it was a blazing inferno. I rushed down to the tree scared to death that the entire island was going to burn.

"Blow!" I screamed to my brother and sister, who were screaming too. "Blow!"

All three trees burned to the ground and that was the end of my great TV series and my father's banana trees.

We also had a couple of large kukuinut trees in our back yard. These are the black nuts which make up the lei that I often wear in performances. In their normal state they look a lot like walnuts—very hard and rough. They are usually kind of a motley gray in color— the color of stainless steel that didn't stay stainless when you used it for your latest project in the basement. Each nut has to be filed and sanded down until it's smooth. In the old days before metal files and electric sanding machines, this used to take forever. After the nut is smooth, the meat from the kukui (another one, of course) is rubbed into it and the nut is buffed. The meat is very oily, so it brings out the black shininess from deep within the nut.

During the days of the monarchy, only those of royal birth could wear these highly polished nuts, because they were so difficult to make. They're not so rare today, of course, and many people will wear these highly prized nuts on special occasions. I like to tell people that I wear them because I'm a child of the King of Kings—but I think my friends think I should wear them to signify that God can bring beauty out of any nut!

One day after a wind storm, one of the very large kukuinut trees was blown over in our back yard. So I got a gang of kids to come over and play "war." I was the general and planned the entire battle.

Two forts were used; the large tree trunk was one and the other a large cardboard crate. Both sides readied their slingshots and loaded them with the rock-hard kukuinuts. I gave the command and the bullets started to fly. For hours we shot those deadly things, but by the grace of God not one found its mark

The news of the missionaries' murder by the Auca Indians was very exciting to me as a boy. There were moments of sadness when I thought of the families who were left behind but that was overpowered by the thrill of bows and arrows and jungle war.

I began making bows and arrows so the gang could have a missionary war. The arrows were real and would have been deadly if they had found their targets. But praise the Lord not one did. I guess I didn't make very good arrows and bows.

I was in the fourth grade when I started delivering papers. I had about fifty homes on my paper route, and they covered an area of about two and one half miles, all over very hilly country. I mention this because there were a couple of areas on the route where I thought very rich people lived. I suppose in comparison to the way people live here on the mainland, they were just average. Most of the people there were *haole* (caucasian), and they weren't very friendly. But one of these families were the Parkers; they were older and whenever I would go on collection I saved them for last. They would invite me in to watch television and to give me a snack.

There were a lot of dogs along the route, so I often got bit. I'd save pieces of bread from my lunch and when the dog would come roaring around the corner after me, I'd whip out this piece of bread, throw it at the dog and say, "In Jesus' Name!" Believe me, I escaped a lot of bites that way.

But the things that really made a difference about my childhood were the spiritual experiences I had. As I look back, I realize how strict my parents were. But that was good because it gave me a sense of the divine presence of God, that I can't go anywhere without God's knowledge. So I was well prepared for the years to come.

3

Teen Years

In high school, you weren't anybody if you couldn't play sports and the big heroes were those who were in sports. I couldn't do anything. I could hardly hit the ball and to top it off I couldn't go down to the community gym like the other kids. By the time I got through seventh grade and went to gym class, they were all dribbling that ball and tossing baskets like a bunch of pros—all I could do was miss.

Now if a *haole* wasn't good in sports, you'd think, *Well, they're haoles, you know they can't do anything.* But a local person was supposed to be able to do it and it was really a disgrace that I couldn't. So I got a lot of razzing which made me feel bad.

So by the time I got into the eighth grade I didn't have anything in common with the other kids. One of my worst times in school was the short recess period. We would stand around the halls and all the kids would talk about their Boy Scout troops, about their Little League, about bowling, or YMCA parties, or all about the latest movies. Well, there wasn't anything I could talk about because I couldn't do any of those things, either because we were too poor or because we weren't allowed to do them. I was the most talkative person there, but I didn't have anything to talk about, and every time I tried to say something, the kids would look at me and laugh.

I thought, *What can I do that nobody else can do? Well, I know one thing—I can sing! I don't know any other man or boy in this entire city who can sing as well as I can.* So I borrowed a Mario Lanza record from the library and asked the librarian for books on how to sing.

The only book they had at that time was one on teaching little boys' choirs. I took the book and the Mario Lanza album home. At that time my brother and I took weekly turns washing dishes. During my week to do the dishes, I closed the kitchen door, closed all the windows, and turned on the Mario Lanza record, brought the speaker into the kitchen, and tried to imitate him.

One of the things I immediately realized was that I didn't have a vibrato. Well, you're not going to sing unless you have a vibrato; all the good singers had vibratos. I told myself that that was the first thing I had to learn to do. I stood at the sink and made my breath come in short spurts: *ahaaaaaaaaa* . . . I would hit my stomach to produce *ehh-ehh-ahh-ahh*. Soon I had what I thought was a pretty good vibrato, but it probably sounded like an old Model T trying to get started.

One Sunday the pastor's son, Charles, got up to sing a solo. He didn't tell me he was going to do something like that; he didn't tell anybody anything. Everybody was enthralled. But what nobody knew was that I had been practicing all this time and I wasn't going to tell anyone either. Of course my parents thought this was another of my crazy ideas, like burning down banana trees.

After the service that Sunday, I went to the pastor and said, "Look, can I sing a solo next Sunday night?" That was unheard of, nobody ever asked. But Charles sang, so I was going to sing, too.

I practiced and practiced. Sunday night finally arrived and I got up to sing "The Love of God". I was so proud of my newly-wrought vibrato. And everybody was amazed—two soloists hatched in two weeks!

That was the beginning and by the time I was a sophomore in high school, I was recognized as a pretty good singer.

I sang my first solo in high school at a Christmas program; Charles sang too. The teacher had one portion of the concert set aside for soloists, and Charles and I were the only ones who got encores. I sang, "Torna Surriento" (Come Back to Surrento). For the encore I sang, "On the Street Where You Live"—with a high A at the end!

I haven't been a tenor all my life. I sang baritone through high school and most of college, because I thought tenors were sissies. I took the baritone leads in *South Pacific* and *Oklahoma* in my junior and senior years in high school, and all the bass solos in the Christmas portion of the *Messiah*.

I had a difficult time changing from baritone to tenor because I was singing wrong. When I was a junior in high school, I won a summer trip with Youth For Christ to Winona Lake Conference—seven weeks of traveling with the Hawaii Youth For Christ director, Dr. Herb Tyler. Those were seven of the most fantastic weeks of my life! It was one time when I was number one top guy, and was with people who understood me and were motivated in the same way I was. When we were in Cleveland, Ohio, at a big Youth For Christ rally, I came out on stage and gave a testimony. I said I was going to sing for them, "It Took A Miracle". I started . . . "My Father is omnipotent . . ." and everybody started to laugh. I talked in such a high pipsqueaky voice but sang in a deep thick bass voice.

When I was in the eighth grade, about three of us in the youth department got burdened for the young people in our church. Before every service (I don't know how I got into this but it shows how the Lord had His hand on my life), we would go downstairs to the bathroom or one of the Sunday school rooms and pray. We asked God to really move in our church.

Soon a revival started and continued for the next eight years. During my high school years, Glad Tidings Assembly averaged maybe 115 in Sunday school and sixty to seventy of them were young people. We were leaders in most of the Christian activities that went on in the city. Many of us were soloists in the band as well as in the choir in school. After I graduated from high school, a lot of the top kids in school were from our church. It all started by going down to the basement and praying before the services.

Our theme at Young People's for a three-month period was, "Win a Friend and Win a Soul." I knew only one kid from the church who went to my school. Here we were supposed to "win a friend and win a soul," and I didn't have any friends at all!

That really bothered me; at night I would cry and cry and beg, "Lord, how can I win anybody to You? When I don't even have any friends?" So I started to watch people around me to see what they did that made people like them. I still think that's a great way to develop character.

Anyway, the only other kid from the church who was in junior high school was Paul. Paul and I made a pact that we would witness to at least one person every week. You cannot believe how hard that was for me, because when I didn't have anybody who would even talk to me, how was I going to witness to them?

I would randomly pick a kid in one of my classes, go up to him and real official-like, say, "Hey, can I meet you after school today?"

"Well," he'd say, "why? What's happening?"

"Well, I'd just like to talk to you about something."

"Well, what'd you want to talk about?"

"Oh, something real serious!" And that's how I witnessed to my classmates, After that three-month period was over, Paul and I didn't have our pact anymore and I was very relieved.

Now, at our church, they had altar calls all the time. After they'd give the altar call for sinners, they'd open up the altar for anyone who wanted to come to pray. I think that's one of the most beautiful things that a church can do—just allow people to come forward and pray. This was a regular thing at our church. We rarely had a dismissal or benediction. It was understood that when people came forward to pray, if you wanted to go home you could go home, or you could stay as long as you wanted to and pray. And it was not unusual, at Friday night youth service, for us kids to be there until way after midnight praying for our friends, weeping and interceding for them all. I know of very few churches that do this regularly. And that's sad.

When we were kids, we'd go up to the altar and pray for about five minutes. Then we'd get up and go back, sit down and wait for our parents to finish praying so we could go home or go to the Dairy Queen. But as we got older it became more and more valuable for us to be "spiritual." We would try to stay at the altar as long as we could. I wouldn't get up until Charles got up, and vice versa. Maybe the motivation was wrong, but God had lots of time to do things, When someone was weeping before the Lord, a couple of kids would get up and go pray with him. It was beautiful to see the kids ministering to others like that, but actually most of the time the reason we did that was because we just wanted to be where the action was.

But God did so many things. I'm saying this because on one side maybe some of the missionaries weren't all that wise. Yet those experiences in the church and the tender, sensitive way in which Pastor and Mrs. Funk ministered to us laid the spiritual foundation of my life.

Sister Funk would play the piano softly and Brother Funk would walk up and down the platform and say, "Lord, bless these children. Bless Mark, fill him with Your Spirit . . . ." He'd walk up and down, blessing each one. Every once in a while, he'd break into a chorus.

If nothing else, it was great group therapy. The fact is that it was a lot more than just good psychology. God met us there. What we had there was group theology.

When I was in high school, I started a Youth For Christ club, and I was president of the club for most of my high school years. This gave me an outlet. We'd make up little jingles to promote the club during the morning announcements. I'd paraphrase "Bloody Mary" from *South Pacific,* changing it to: "Dum, dum, dum! YFC is the place to be . . . dum, dum, dum . . . ." Then it ended up, "Don't be a dum-dum! Be at YFC." I don't think it attracted anybody to the club, but we sure had fun.

During my junior year I was able to do more and more witnessing among the kids—especially kids in chorus. Most of the kids who joined chorus were rejects from other classes. They couldn't take two study halls so they took chorus. It was just an easy credit.

I became very close to some of these kids and this was

the first time I had any real friends who didn't also go to my church. One of them (we called him Gorilla because he looked like one) was the ugliest person I thought I had ever seen just a huge hulk of a guy. Everybody was kind of scared of him.

One day we were sitting in chorus and Gorilla had just come out from behind the gym where they all did their smoking. The chorus room was on that side of the gym. He had cigarette odor all over him.

"Hey, church boy," he said teasingly, "how come you no smoke, eh?" I was scared of him, but I said, "Why? You want to give me a cigarette? If you teach me how, I will." I wouldn't have done it, but I wanted to see what he'd say.

He looked at me and his eyes got all watery. He put his big arm around me and said, "Hey, Eddy, don't ever let me catch you smoking." From that time on, Gorilla was my personal bodyguard.

During my senior year, I was president of the chorus—that didn't mean a whole lot to the rest of the school because the chorus wasn't a big deal. Most of the kids in chorus were rugged, Hawaiian "rednecks." About a week before an unprecedented performance of the *Messiah* (no one thought a bunch of flunkies like us could do it), the kids were acting up in rehearsal. The director said, "Well, just forget it! We won't do it!" and walked out.

I got up in front of the kids and proceeded to tell them what a bunch of so-and-so's I thought they were. Nobody ever talked to those kids like that and got away with it. "If you cut me up in little pieces and beat me up and leave me all over the ground," I said, "I will still tell you that you are all stupid idiots! Acting like little children!"

We had a rehearsal scheduled during lunch recess.

"Now I'm going to be there," I said, "and you had better be there. I'm going to direct you and we're going to do this concert whether Mr Battles is there or not." So I took my "Messiah" score to English class and practiced conducting while the teacher taught prepositions. The chorus members all showed up that recess and I had my first directing experience. The actual performance was a smash.

I didn't have a whole lot going for me except a big mouth and some charisma or something. The Lord was preparing me for times ahead. I became a leader in the chorus.

Mr. Battles, the director, was the first black man I knew; his was the only black family on the entire island. When they introduced him, when he first came to school, the student body gave him a standing ovation. That was when they were having those troubles in Alabama. He was embarrassed, but the kids thought he was the toughest person around.

One day I asked him, "Mr. Battles, why am I so lonely? I want friends so much, but I don't have anybody who is a personal friend of mine. I'm Gorilla's friend, I'm Bozo's friend, but I feel more like a big daddy to these guys. I want someone to be my friend."

"Eddy," he said, "you were destined since your birth to be a leader. All leaders are lonely. You will be lonely all your life."

But I said, "I don't want to be lonely. I don't want to be a leader."

"You don't have any choice, that's the way you are," he said. You will always be out in front. That's just the way you're going to be."

I've never forgotten that, and it's been true. I have since met others in leadership positions who also lead lonely lives. And God has given me a sense of fellowship with some of them.

All my life I'd wanted a close friend, someone I could talk to and share with, someone who wouldn't laugh at me, someone who would really stick with me. Charles told me one time that what I needed was a girl friend. I had several girl friends, but it wasn't there.

There was a big mango tree way up in the back of the bushes behind our house. I would go out to this mango tree and talk to it and share deep things. The mango tree didn't ever recoil in horror, nor did it immediately put me at the top of its prayer list. It didn't blab around to everybody. It just listened.

During one of those times when I was talking to the Lord, I said, "Lord, it really must be nice to sit up there with Your gold streets and with those big pearl gates, and all the angels. I mean You have everything You need. You don't ever get real down in the dumps and lonely like I do, do You?"

"Yes, I do," the Lord said.

"You do?" I asked. "I thought you had everything! You don't need anything."

"Yes, I do," He said. "I do need something."

I thought, *He couldn't possibly know how I feel. He's just trying to make me feel good.*

His answer was, "I need you!" I need you to love, and I need you to love Me."

Can you imagine that? The Lord ministered to me under that mango tree. He told me that as long as He was lonely for me, I would always be lonely — and nobody and nothing would ever fill that loneliness; no girl friend, no money, no friends, no success, no nothing. And no matter how popular I became, no matter how well-accepted I was, no matter whether I became a football hero or whatever, I would never really feel accepted and fulfilled until His loneliness for my love was filled. A lot of people are offended at the thought that God needs us — that God has a need at all. The sovereignty of God precludes any need that He could have. But my God really needs me. That's why He created me — to love me. Otherwise He could love His angels. He could express Himself and His love to rose bushes, or poodles or diamonds and rubies. And they would all probably be a lot more accommodating than most of us are. But angels and roses and poodles and jewels cannot love Him like people can. We are His highest expression of creativity — created in His very image. The essence of His very being is love and we, being in His image, are made so that we are fulfilled when we respond to His love, His forever aloha.

I think God could relate to me like this because I so much needed the personal fellowship of a friend. I was very popular in high school and everybody needed me, but they didn't realize that I needed them. So everybody came to me with their problems but I couldn't tell anybody my problems. That's been the story of my life. That's the way it was in church; that's the way it was in college and now that's the way it is in our ministry. Sure, a lot of people say, "Come on, Mark, you can share with us." But as soon as I begin, they don't quite know how to handle it. They either feel disillusioned, shocked, self-righteous, or sorry.

It was partly my burden for my friends in school and partly my need for fellowship and acceptance that caused me to go out of my way to witness to my friends at school. I knew that I would not really have fellowship with them unless they had fellowship with me. And I knew I could never have fellowship with them until they knew Jesus! Since I couldn't go to their parties I got them to come to mine.

4
College Days

When the time came for me to go to college, I was so naive I didn't know that I was supposed to apply to the school and pre-register. If you think that was dumb—I didn't register for the draft until after my nineteenth birthday for the same reason. I thought they came and looked for you. It was August before I realized that I didn't know where I was going to school. I applied to the University of Hawaii and fortunately I was accepted. I didn't apply anywhere else because there was no other university and I couldn't afford to go to the mainland.

The university was in Oahu, Hawaii (Honolulu), about 200 air miles from Hilo, so I had to leave the people I had grown up with.

I was already a "father-knows-best" figure to the young people in our church. During that last summer how close I felt to these kids, how emotionally involved I was with them.

I had a summer choir at the church—that was the first real choir I directed. All my best friends were in the choir and we were rehearsing to do a special song, Audrey Mieir's arrangement of Stuart Hamblen's "How

Big Is God?". (It is one of the songs Diane and I sing in our concerts today.)

It was going to be the last Sunday morning I would be there to direct the choir. We had a rehearsal on Thursday night, and without telling me a word, about nine of the guys went skating instead of coming to practice. Of course I could not have choir practice with hardly any of the guys there. I was crushed that they would do something like that—and they hadn't even invited me to go with them. They skipped out on the one night that was really important to me. I think it was an overreaction or an unconscious reaction to the fact that I wasn't going to be there anymore. Kind of a breaking away from their dependence on me.

The Lord taught me a good lesson through that. I spent most of the night at the church weeping because I had been so hurt. It could have been anybody else, but these were nine of my closest friends. They didn't understand how it was going to hurt me because they figured, "Nothing hurts Mark." They didn't know!

So I cried in the dark basement of the church in one of the Sunday school rooms. During that lonely hour the song, "Does Jesus Care?", came to my mind: "Does Jesus care when my heart is pained?" Now, can you imagine that as a kid who was just being turned on with Ralph Carmichael's music—"Does Jesus Care?" just wasn't one of the in-hymns. The whole song floated back to me . . . "Though my tears flow all the night long . . . And my sad heart aches till it nearly breaks . . . ." The chorus seemed to swell through the room as if all the angels were singing right into my ears: "Oh, yes, He cares; I know He cares. His heart is touched with my grief."

His heart is *touched*—another notch in the theology God was trying to teach me about how deeply He loves me. He wasn't just concerned with me as a social service person, but His heart was *touched* with *my* grief! Not because the kids didn't show up for choir rehearsal (He knew that was going to turn out okay), and not because the kids went skating. He was sad because I was sad.

Next morning the guys called me and told me they couldn't sleep because the Lord had convicted their hearts. When the pastor had heard how hurt I was, he had gone down to the skating rink, didn't say a word—just walked in on them. The boys said as soon as he walked in, it was as if God had said, "Harumph!" They all stopped skating and knew immediately they had done wrong.

Sunday morning the choir sang "How Big Is God?", and I sang the solo part.

It was the custom of the church, when anybody was going to leave, to gather in the front, join hands to encircle the person, and sing a song that said, "Aloha, may you know His peace. . . ." (That song was written by Bertha Mae Blair for the young people in our church.) So they gathered around me: the kids I had led to the Lord, the ones God has used to teach me many valuable lessons, and some kids I didn't even know. That meant so much to me because it was the end of a whole era of my life.

During my first semester in college, in November, I received a birthday card from the kids at the church. One of the names on the card was "Donald." The only Donald I knew was a kid I had been praying for for three years, five minutes every day. But when I left home, he wasn't near to coming to the Lord. In December I got a Christmas card and again I saw the name "Donald."

When I went home for Christmas vacation, I asked my friends, "Who is this Donald?"

"It's the Donald you've been praying for for three years!" they said.

That was another notch in my life, to remind me that God is dependable. It doesn't make any difference what happens around me, how successful I am, or even whether I'm pulling the strings to make things happen, I know He is faithful. He loves me and always keeps His word.

My college years were uneventful, except that I didn't have many friends. The first semester I was so "out of it" that I didn't know where I was or going. Everybody was into joining fraternities, and I wasn't into that sort of thing.

The one shining light of my first years in college was one of the freshman boys. The Sunday after President Kennedy was shot, this boy to whom I'd been witnessing, came to the church and accepted Christ as his Savior.

As a result, Ronald was instrumental in leading about thirty kids in the music department to the Lord. By the end of my sophomore year, we had a large prayer group in the music department. That added strength to my Christian life.

During the latter part of my freshman year at the University I became involved in the Inter-Varsity Christian Fellowship. This got me into the Word on my own by inductive Bible study. I didn't make any fantastic personal discoveries then, but at least it laid the groundwork for discoveries I would make in the future.

During the rest of my years at college I was a Bible study leader. I never had any other Bible training.

During my junior year, I entered the Metropolitan Opera auditions, I didn't win anything significant until the next year, 1967, when I won the Metropolitan Opera auditions for the Pacific. I had the privilege of going to New York and competing there for a week, at the end of which I decided opera wasn't for me. I wasn't able to sit all the way through any opera except *La Boheme*. Everybody and everything there seemed so plastic to me. The whole thing seemed like human jukeboxes—drop in enough money and people keep singing songs; if they don't keep singing, the money stops coming. Human values and humanity seemed to mean very little. It was whatever money could buy. I felt as though I were in a singer's farmer's market.

Of course the competition was spooky, as any competition is, but I was young and stupid. I didn't know the grand nature of opera. (Even today I'm sure I don't understand the whole thing.) So I just sang my songs the best I knew how. The only thing I was concerned about was that I didn't blow the top notes.

By this time I had switched from baritone to tenor. It was during my junior year that my regular voice teacher, Dick Vine, took a semester's leave of absence. The new voice teacher, Bud Remley, was a retired voice teacher from New York. He started me up the scale until I said, "Um, I don't sing that high."

"Well, why not?" he asked.

"Because I'm a baritone," I said.

"Like ---- you are!" he said. And that was the end of that. I sang tenor from that time on. But for a long time I sang tenor with a baritone production, so I didn't develop as quickly as I could have.

All I was concerned about was that I could do well enough so I wouldn't be ashamed, be embarrassed. But it was Mr. Remley who took me by the shoulder more than once and said, "Young man, you could one day become one of the world's greatest tenors. No, you could be the greatest tenor who ever lived."

I never quite knew how to handle that. I would just laugh nervously, thank him and leave.

I'll never know whether or not that could have been true. Sometime later, after we had already been in the Aloha ministry on the mainland, when I was questioning the wisdom of the path we had chosen (the sheer physical demands of our kind of work deny any real vocal development), the Lord seemed to say to me, "Mark, the world had heard all the greatest singers. You are not to compete for a place on the top of that very steep and narrow mountain. I have chosen you to sing with far more than your vocal chords—to sing a song of love that cannot be heard with human ears, and to teach that song to people who couldn't carry a tune in a bucket!"

The aria I sang in competition in New York was "Questa o guella" from Verdi's *Rigoletto*. It was suggested that I sing that one because it's one of the earliest arias in the book and my voice was a bit underdeveloped.

I was such a little boy. Here I was going to get married a month after I got back and was still so naive that I spent the entire six days in New York in my hotel room unless I was doing something over at the Center. I didn't know how to catch a cab, and I was afraid to try.

About this time I got a phone call from a Congregational church. The Congregational churches are part of the United Church of Christ, the largest denomination in Hawaii. Most of them are quite liberal, but this particular church was evangelical. They asked me to become their music director, so that meant I could go to a different church. The reason the Lord wanted me there was that He knew the ministry He had planned for us there. We would not have fit into all the Methodist,

Lutheran, Baptist and other churches if I had not had that experience.

My father has written only a few letters to me in my entire life. One was after my first semester in college. I had decided to quit college and go to a Bible school that the rest of my friends were attending in California. He wrote and said, "Stay in college." His advice was right. Although he was a minister, he said, "Stay in a secular school; don't go to a Christian school." Somehow he knew that the experience I was going to receive would be very valuable to me in the future. Had I gone to a Christian school, I don't think I would have been prepared for this ministry. My secular education taught me to think and analyze, and not just accept traditions I had been raised in.

Another time he replied to a letter I wrote him about how disillusioned I was. He said I should just stick it out and the Lord would take care of me. He said that it wasn't so much the church as it was my relationship with God that needed straightening out.

During my senior year in college I practice-taught at Roosevelt High School in Honolulu. The chorus was made up primarily of Hawaiian kids who were from the "Hawaiian reservation"—land that was set aside exclusively for native Hawaiians. During this time I began to be involved with bringing kids over to the house.

One of the first was a student named Dwight. He was a big husky Hawaiian kid on the football team who carried a lot of weight around school. Like a lot of the Hawaiian kids, he wasn't very academically inclined, but he sure liked to have fun. And he often got into mischief pursuing that fun. I got along well with all the students but several of them seemed to be more open, sincere and responsive. Dwight was one of these. So I spent quite a bit of extra time and energy encouraging him and in just "being there."

One day, while walking to school, I saw him drive by in the opposite direction. Dwight stopped the car and ran up to me to explain, "Mr. Yasuhara, we're going to see the doctor."

Soon after I arrived at school I got a note from the office saying that these kids had cut class. I didn't mind them cutting class—kids do that. But Dwight had deliberately lied to me, and that hurt.

I prayed and prayed. That night at about ten-thirty, Dwight knocked on my apartment door. He had walked about two and a half miles to get there. He came in and choked and slobbered out an apology; he was really broken up. That night I led Dwight to the Lord.

During the course of that year, I was impressed with the effectiveness of loving, caring, sometimes firm relationships that could be forged between teachers and their oft-times distrusting, disappointing, frustrating students. And that some of these worst offenders were often the most responsive to real love.

I was having a hard time financially. I wasn't eligible for more government loans. I needed money so I took out a short-term, three-month loan. There was no way that I was going to be able to pay back the loan on my $100 a month income. I could have gotten a job, except that I was involved with so many music activities which were a part of my training.

One Sunday morning I was rushing into choir practice and Ike stopped me and said, "Mark, I've got talk to you."

"Can it wait until afterward?" I asked.

"No, I have got to talk with you right now," he said.

Reluctantly I went to his car with him. He turned to

me and said, "Mark, I was closing the cash register last night and every night I go through the same type of ritual. I say to the Lord, 'Lord, how much of this money do You want me to have; how much do You want to take?' And whatever money the Lord said He wanted, that's the money I took out.

"Well, the Lord told me last night to take out all the bills from this certain compartment and give them to Mark. I haven't counted them yet, but here they are."

He handed me the brown paper bag and said, "Here, you count it, for the Lord said it was all yours."

Well, you know how much it amounted to? You're right, it came to a little over $350. Exactly what I needed. Praise the Lord!

During my senior year one of the music professors came to see me one day and said, "Mark, I understand you do quite a bit of singing in churches and such."

I said, "Yes."

"Well, I'm sure you realize that a musician of quality must have real discrimination in the kind of music he chooses to sing," he said. "There's an awfully lot of sweet, sick sentimentality floating around in Christian music."

"Oh? Like what?" I asked.

He said, "For instance, that silly little ditty that goes something like, 'And He walks with me and He talks with me, and tells me I am His own.' Now that is ridiculous. It is so soupy, sentimental . . . it nauseates me."

I didn't want to be sweet, sick and sentimental, but at the same time I was being challenged by every Christian musician, it seemed.

Songs such as, "Every day with Jesus is sweeter than the day before." Now what does that mean? Perhaps a deeper experience—but not sweeter. As a twenty-one-year-old college senior I knew that not many of my days were necessarily sweeter than the day before. So I took that one out of my repertoire and didn't sing a lot of those songs for a long time. In fact, I didn't sing "In the Garden" again until almost three years later. Now it is one of our most-loved popular songs.

During the second semester of my junior year, I began having a Bible study with several of the kids in the church. Soon they seemed to come alive for the Lord; these kids were going to be the leaders of the church in the future. One of the boys of this group was Fran. The only time I could have Bible study with him was on Wednesday night during the mid-week service.

I prayed about it and decided to go ahead. You should have heard the flack I got! "You're being a bad influence on the other young people—a bad example by not being in prayer meeting." (Not a whole lot of kids went to prayer meeting!) "I don't care what you have to do, you should be in church when there's service, your place is always there." "What makes you think that you're better than the rest of us? If you want Fran to have a Bible study, see that he's in church on Wednesday night." (Fran hadn't been attending mid-week service, anyway.)

This came as a bomb to me. Until that time I had been superintendent of the junior high department and was directing one of the choirs which I had gotten together myself. I was active in Inter-Varsity, I was bringing friends to church, and I was doing this and that, just working myself into the ground . . . a real martyr. And now after all I was doing for the church and "the Lord," my sincerity and basic Christian integrity were being questioned on the basis of whether I went to the Wednesday night prayer meeting. All I was doing was having a Bible study with a kid who wouldn't have gone to the service anyway.

That turned me off and this, of course, happened when most of my generation were challenging any kind of authority at all. The hippie movement had started when I entered college. It wasn't that I was rebelling against authority; I just felt intimidated, underrated and misunderstood.

There were several things that hurt. It occurred to me that I was not being accepted, loved and appreciated as a person on the basis of who I was but on what I did for a program.

I began to realize that many of the friends I thought I had—relationships I thought I had, real spiritual relationships I had acquired in my three years in college—were often based on what I was doing for them. If I didn't lead Bible studies, if I didn't take charge of recreation at camp, if I refused to do whatever I was asked by the church, I risked placing my Christianity in question. So I just tried to go to all the meetings and do everything because I was asked to. I wanted them to know I was sincere and was a "good Christian."

About this time, I seriously considered the alternative to going to church, but I don't mean I considered going all out for the devil. I didn't want to leave; I didn't want to be out of the fellowship. I wasn't rebelling, I was being pushed out of the fellowship. So many kids feel that way. It's often not the attraction of evil that gets to them. It's the unattractiveness, the mickey mouse bitterness in the fellowship that turns them off, and in over-reaction, they rebel and throw in the towel.

In my case I didn't do anything overt. I just stopped going to church. But did I miss it, it was terrible.

One night I did go to the Sunday night service. After everybody had left and the lights had been turned out, I found a little hideout between the third and fourth pews in the sanctuary, knelt and had it out with the Lord. I cried and prayed, "Lord, after all I have done, look at what's happening. Please, give me a word. Please give me something just for me right now."

Immediately I heard myself say, "The Lord is my shepherd, I shall not want!" I stopped and said, "Lord, don't give me some of that old-fashioned stuff. I need something new and fresh I don't want any of that old trite verbage."

So I prayed again, and again I heard myself say, "The Lord is my Shepherd, I shall not want!"

I felt stupid. I thought the Lord had taken the side of all those bigoted, narrow-minded saints and that He was telling me I'd just have to settle down into the same old rut.

One more time it happened: "The Lord is my shepherd, I shall not want." By this time I was saying it out loud, real loud and all the time. I just cried and cried. Then the Lord spoke to me again. "Mark," He said, "if I really was your shepherd, you wouldn't want."

"But You are! You are my shepherd, Lord. All my life I have tried to follow You," I cried.

Then I heard myself say, "He maketh me to lie down in green pastures." By this time I was listening closely; this was the first time this had ever happened to me. It was kind of spooky.

The Lord said to me in my head, just as He had at the mango tree many years before, "Every pasture I have led you to has been green whether you knew it or not. Maybe you didn't like the kind of grass. Lots of times you don't even know whether it's a pasture at all. You fuss and complain and whine. Or else, you'll say, 'Oh look at the beautiful pasture,' and you run all around the place and jump up and down! Besides, you tend to be color-blind; you don't know whether it's green, brown or red. So if you just assume that wherever I put you is a green pasture, that's all you need to know. So just lie down."

Then came: "He leadeth me beside still waters."

He said, "Mark, every time I lead you by the still waters, instead of doing as you're told and gently go *beside* the water, you jump in and splash around. You want to have a great big glory hallelujah time. Now you listen to me! If I tell you to jump in, jump in. But if want to lead you beside the water, you stay out of things. No wonder you're forever catching spiritual pneumonia!"

Finally we got to: "He leadeth me into paths of righteousness for His name's sake."

"Mark," the Lord said, "it's not for your church's sake, it's not for your folks' sake, it's not for your spiritual reputation's sake. It's for My name's sake. So all the paths I lead you into are paths of righteousness—for my name's sake."

Later on, I found that Paul had learned to be content wherever he was and that everything works together for good. But that night was a turning point in my life as far as to whom I would answer. I began to get the feeling that there was an awful lot of what I thought I was doing for the Lord that was in need of re-evaluation.

So ended my college years and the Lord began to "lead anew."

5
Little Brown Gal Meets Funny Little Guy

I was a senior in high school when I first noticed Mark. I was a member of First Assembly of God in Honolulu. The young people would go down to the YMCA about once a month to have an evening of fun—we'd rent the whole place, the pool, the gym. On one particular Saturday, we were finished with our playing and were standing by the refreshment stand.

Our associate pastor was having a family reunion, and the whole Yasuhara clan was there at the "Y". There were seven brothers altogether, and their wives and children, from the various islands. I was kind of a new member of the church and didn't know who the Yasuharas were, except that several of them were very staunch members of the church.

Most of us kids were near the entrance of the banquet room where they were holding their family reunion. I was facing the door and all of a sudden it swung open. The boy coming out caught my eye; I felt a strange sensation for this person really attracted my attention. It was probably just because I thought he was good looking, but all night long I thought of the boy in the doorway. Who was he, anyway?

The next day was Sunday and, oddly enough, the same person showed up in church. I learned later that all the Yasuharas had decided to stay over and attend our church that Sunday morning. In the middle of the service, an old Japanese lady stood up, just before the pastor was going to speak, and asked him if her grandson could sing a solo. I thought, *Oh, brother, not one of those. I wonder who she means?*

I'll never forget that moment—he sang "It Took A Miracle" in an operatic style. It absolutely floored me because nobody in Hawaii, especially none of the local people I knew, could sing like that. Almost everyone in Hawaii gets out his ukulele or his guitar and sings, but no one sings like that.

For some reason I had always been interested in classical music. When I was a little girl, my aunt took me to all the concerts at the concert hall. So out of the entire family I was the only one who liked classical music. Now I asked around until I found out that this boy's name was Edward Mark and that he liked to be called Mark.

I was so excited when I discovered that he was going to attend the university. He spent his first six months out in the country living with a family there. Then during his second semester he lived with his uncle who was the assistant pastor of our church, so he naturally came to our church. Soon we got to know each other through the music of the church. He said that he had noticed me on the Sunday morning he had sung the solo—this soprano voice in the choir, but he couldn't see me because I was so short and the pulpit was in the way.

Our first date was at my senior banquet, the year I graduated from high school. He offered to take me to the banquet if I would pay my own way. You read it right—I had to pay my own way. To top it off, he was an hour late. He sent someone else to pick me up, take me to the banquet, and then he showed up at the banquet an hour later—that was some date! I was mad, but the sight of him changed that quickly. Both of us were very much into music, so through that, we were thrown together quite a bit.

I thought Mark had very strange ideas about boy-girl relationships. For example, he would hardly hold my hand, let alone kiss me. However, we continued to date quite a bit. How I wanted him to hold my hand and give me a good-night kiss once in awhile. I suppose this was because I wasn't raised in a Christian home and couldn't understand some of his ideas.

My parents tell me that they met in church and that they attended church for awhile. But when we children came along all I can remember is that they sent us to Sunday school and church. Maybe once or twice they went with us. As a result, when I became old enough to say that I didn't want to go, I didn't. Eventually we all stopped going to church.

Then during my sophomore year in high school, my brother was discharged from the Air Force and came home for awhile—he was on his way to the mission field in Thailand. He told us he had come home for the specific purpose of sharing the claims of Christ with us. He had always been a Christian, I thought. He was always a good boy—never gave my parents any trouble, and always helped them out. But he told us he really was not a Christian until he went into the Air Force. He shared with us how his sergeant had led him to the Lord and that while he was in the Air Force, the Lord had called him to be a missionary.

I remember him sitting in the living room and trying to tell us about the Lord and how much He meant to him. It just went over the top of my head; I couldn't grasp what he was talking about. Then one Sunday evening, he took me to the church where he was going to speak. To this day I can't remember what he talked about, but it was something I responded to. When he asked who wanted to give their hearts to the Lord, my hand was the first to go up. All I could do was cry, so I went forward and accepted Christ as my Savior. You could say that I cried and repented my way to Jesus.

This was what I had been looking for all the time, but didn't know it. Mark has already talked about loneliness, and to some degree that's the same kind of feeling I had all through junior high, and until that point in high school. You know how girls are—they want to be part of a large group, be popular and have close friends. But I had this inferiority complex too. A lot of it had to do with my weight problem. I had always been overweight, ever since I can remember.

How thankful I was that my brother cared enough about us to share Christ. That was the most important day of my life.

When I went home that night with my brother and told my parents what had happened, I can't remember any negative reaction from them. Even though they didn't go to church, they were not opposed to Christianity. So they just kind of accepted it, which is the way most people are in Hawaii. They're not Christians, but neither are they really Buddhists or anything else; they just live good lives. They don't want to do anything wrong. Many of them no longer have any real religious traditions that they uphold.

My brother told my parents the news that he was going to be a missionary. They didn't object to the fact that he was going to be a missionary; their objection was that missionaries don't earn a lot of money. So financially he wouldn't be very secure, and I think that's the only thing my parents objected to. They realized that he was doing something good so they were proud of him.

Most Oriental families are structured so that the children are raised to be independent and to think for themselves. So it was with my brothers and sisters. My parents raised all of us to think independently so we could survive on our own. Because of this, they hardly ever interfered in our lives. When Mark and I decided to come to the mainland to do what we are doing, they didn't actually like it because we would be far from home. I know they have worried about our well-being, but they never objected.

That's the philosophy of the Oriental: Raise your children to do right and when they are on their own, the parent has the confidence they will make the right decisions.

So I didn't grow up with a lot of the ideas that Mark did. As I said before, he wouldn't even hold my hand because he didn't want to be a stumbling block to the kids who were younger than we. He wouldn't even sit with me in church. He was already in college and I was out of high school. Can you imagine? He wouldn't sit with me in church because he didn't want the other kids to get the same idea, but that's the way he was. I thought it was so strange. But I really didn't care, I knew he would be mine someday!

One day we realized that we couldn't do anything about our relationship for at least another two or three years, until Mark graduated from college. We wanted to be practical; we didn't want to get married until he graduated and had a job. So we decided that we would not date each other for an entire year to see if this was really love and of the Lord. And we did just that for a whole year. He dated other girls and I dated other guys. A year later we decided that the Lord was really in it—and I had lost about twenty-five pounds! We got married the year he graduated from college.

    I can remember praying, when I first became a Christian, about my life's mate. I asked the Lord for somebody unusual (I don't know why I did that). I just prayed that the Lord would give me somebody different. I didn't know what I was asking for. He took me at my word and gave me Mark!

6
Together

Diane and I spent almost the entire three years of our courtship on a motor scooter. To the people of Honolulu, we must have really looked a sight. Honolulu is a very large city, comparable to Atlanta or Houston, skyscrapers and all. So two kids dressed in formal wear, buzzing down the main drag of town, caught the eyes of a few to be sure. Diane would sit sidesaddle, holding her long black hair, and away we would go, singing at the top of our voices.

Many times people ask us how and when do we practice all the songs we sing. Believe it or not, I would say we learned about a third of our songs on the motor scooter while driving around Honolulu.

Sometimes though, I got to borrow Diane's dad's car. I knew the good romantic spots on the island and we would drive there and park and practice our songs. Honest! Some of our best songs, such as "Guide Me, O Thou Great Jehovah", were rehearsed in those lover's lanes.

I guess the first time that Diane and I talked about marriage was one evening on top of the Kahala Hilton Hotel. Many times we would take the elevator to the roof and watch the stars and the beautiful Hawaiian moon. We couldn't afford to go to the restaurant there, so this was our way of having an inexpensive but romantic time. Diane had just returned from a three-month tour of California with a trio. I had spent the summer traveling with a boys' trio throughout the Islands, singing at children's crusades and revival meetings.

We both decided that night, at the top of the Kahala Hilton, that the last thing we would ever do should we get married was to travel in a singing ministry.

There were several reasons. Number one, we didn't enjoy traveling from place to place to place. We wanted to have a home and didn't like living out of a suitcase. Number two, we didn't like having to meet people and then leave them; we get attached to people. I especially didn't like superficial relationships, so I got deeply involved with the people and then I had to up and leave them. Another reason for not wanting to go into this type of ministry was because we didn't want to be associated with any of the mickey mouse gospel groups who were running around the countryside, taking up offerings, selling records and making a zoo out of the whole thing. We had heard a lot and seen for ourselves some of the all-mouth-and-no-action kind of Christian lives some of these gospel singers lived. Of course this isn't true of all of them, but we'd only heard a lot about the real yo-yo's.

Then there was the fact that I didn't think gospel music had much musical legitimacy. I loved it but thought of it as Christian pop music and I thought that as an educated musician (tut, tut) I had more talent than that.

We were married on the eighteenth of June. The entire wedding ceremony was an analogy between Christ and the Church and Diane and me. It was a beautiful story and Pastor Funk conducted the service as if he was telling a story to a couple of children. Diane and I cried through the whole thing. Both of us were really blessed and so were the others that attended.

Many people ask us if we sang at our own wedding. We didn't because we had sung at so many other people's weddings that we decided that our wedding wasn't going to be a mini-concert spectacle.

We didn't have a lot of money for a big reception. In Hawaii the custom is to have a great big sit-down dinner for the wedding couple. Most people will spend thousands of dollars on the wedding reception. Of course Diane's parents couldn't afford that kind of goings-on and we didn't expect it either. So we told our folks we would handle the entire reception. It was a simple stand-up affair with finger sandwiches and punch made by the ladies of the church.

We wanted the ceremony to be the most important thing so we planned the service so that if the people didn't come to the ceremony they would miss a lot. A lot of people on the Island attend only the wedding reception and don't even bother to go to the service.

The cake was going to be the most expensive thing on the budget. The baker told us that we could have several layers that were only cardboard, so that we could still have a large-looking cake—for a lot less money. So we did just that. But when we started to cut the cake at the reception, we had forgotten that the bottom layer was cardboard. We pushed and pushed. I thought, *What is the matter with this crazy cake?* Everybody was looking at us, wondering what was wrong, when all of a sudden it dawned on us that we were cutting into the cardboard. Without thinking, I exclaimed aloud, "That's the cardboard cake we're cutting into!" Of course everybody heard me, and you can imagine how long it was before we lived that down!

After we were married I taught at the Kamehameha Schools for a year in the general music and choir departments substituting for a woman who was on a maternity leave.

At the end of the year I was offered another year's contract with them with the promise that if anything came up on a permanent basis that I could have first choice. By the way, this school is the sole beneficiary of revenues from the lands of the Kamehamehas, the largest and most powerful monarchy in Hawaii's history and only children of Hawaiian ancestry can go there. There are a lot of blue-eyed blondes that go there though. As long as they had some blood relative way back in the Dark Ages who was a least part Hawaiian, they're eligible. The school is one of the few remaining legacies of the native Hawaiian people and it is always an honor to be associated with it.

At the end of that year my voice was getting hoarse from teaching six to eight classes every day and directing the choir. My voice teacher told me that I was going to have to decide whether I was going to be a teacher or a singer. Because at the rate I was going, with the enthusiasm and intensity that I put into my teaching, I wouldn't have any real facility in my voice much longer.

Evidently this happens to a lot of music teachers. So I thought that instead of taking that second contract I would go away to school and get my master's or maybe my doctorate in vocal performance.

I went to Ike Akamine who was the head of the deacons at the church where I was a member. Ike was now truly a Spirit-filled man of God and only five years before had been an adamant Buddhist. He hadn't liked

Christians at all, but the Lord saved him and filled him with the Holy Spirit.

Ike was at that time a millionaire several times over and owned several successful corporations, the largest of which was a chain of supermarkets. Soon after he became a Christian, Ike became concerned about the selling of liquor in his stores. One day he took all the liquor out of his supermarkets and as a result got into a lot of legal hassles and suits with the liquor companies. In the end, he lost everything he had and had to file for bankruptcy. Through all of this the Lord really grew in Ike. Very few people meet him today, *experience* his booming, deep "Praise the Lord" and come away without sensing that they have been with a spiritual giant.

At the time I went to Ike, he had acquired a souvenir shop down in Waikiki. I asked him if I could borrow some money so I could go back to school.

At this same time there were a couple of important singing jobs in Waikiki that opened up to me. These weren't raunchy night clubs, but nice places where you sang good old-fashiioned Hawaiian songs. The starting pay was about $700 a week which was just out of this world, considering that I was teaching for $650 a month. I told Ike that I had three alternatives: I could accept another teaching contract; I could go back to school; or I could take one of these entertainment opportunities.

"Well, Mark," he said, "I don't have to pray about the third one because I know that the Lord doesn't want you to go into that type of work." Now there are not too many people I would take that from. But for Ike, being the spiritual man that he was, I opened both ears. He continued, "Mark, I just know that God doesn't want you singing in those entertainment places."

I should say a word here that I don't think it is wrong

for a Christian to go into the entertainment field if God has called him specifically to do that. At that particular time of our lives God wasn't calling us to do that, although He has since assured us that had we chosen to do that, He would have still blessed us. But we were really trying to follow him. I think that if the Lord would give us the green light, it would be perfectly all right for us to go back to Hawaii right now and go into the entertainment business. It wouldn't be wrong for us to do it, but His will is for us to do what we are doing.

Anyway, Ike said, "I don't think you should go back to school and I don't think you should..."he paused for a moment and prayed..."sign the contract to teach school next year. The Lord seems to really impress on me that you should keep yourself completely free of any contractual agreements with anyone. The Lord is going to open up a fantastic ministry for you and He wants you to be free so that when He calls you, you will be free to leave right then."

"How am I going to live if I don't work?" I asked. Diane was working, but both of us had to work just to make a living.

Ike then said, "I'll give you $300 every month, $150 every two weeks so you can be free." So I spent the entire summer sewing leis down in his souvenir shop.

During that summer my former roommate, Phil Reed, whom I had led to the Lord during one of the Billy Graham Crusades in Hawaii, had an asthma attack. The doctor had told him if he had many more attacks, one of them would be fatal. One day while walking around in Waikiki he ran out of his asthma medicine. He stumbled into the souvenir shop, wheezing and choking at about four-thirty in the afternoon.

"Mark!" he gasped. "I got to get home quick, I ran out

of my medicine over an hour ago."

So we jumped into my car and drove into the rush hour traffic. It was stop and go, stop and go. I yelled and honked the horn, but nothing worked—the traffic was too heavy.

Phil was pounding and scratching the windows, trying to catch his breath. I knew he was choking to death.

When we got to his apartment, he got out of the car and rushed toward the building, but he collapsed on the sidewalk. He couldn't breathe. I ran to the apartment wondering what I could do there; he had a combination lock on the door. I yelled down the stairs, "Somebody, please come and help me! I think he's dying!"

No one came, so I picked Phil up and put him back in the car. I was in near panic. I raced to the nearest hospital which was about four minutes away. I cried, "Lord, don't let him die." But by the time I got to the hospital, Phil had died, right there in the front seat of my car.

That experience did something to me. I thought, *so young to die.* And I realized how important every second is to us.

Soon after Phil's death Diane and I moved into a large, two-bedroom apartment. How nice, we thought. We would be able to use the one bedroom for an office where we could work on our music and such . . . but the Lord had other plans.

7

A Few Years Older Than Our Son

I met Don Haas while I was a freshman at the University; he was in the East-West Center on a grant from the United States, studying for a master's degree in school administration. He was now vice-principal of another junior high school, and we would get together and talk about what was happening.

In January 1968, we were at his house and Don said, "Mark, I want you to pray with me about a kid." This was unusual because Don had about 600 kids in his school.

"What's the matter?" I said.

"Well, I was walking down the hallway one day and as I stopped in front of one of the classrooms like I so often do, the Lord seemed to turn a spotlight on one kid in the middle of the class. I thought my heart was going to break, and I didn't even know who the kid was. This last week he has been in the office two or three times for a paddling. I feel that God has a special thing planned for this boy."

I told him that I would pray.

In April of that year, Don sent Fred to a Christian

camp. Fred accepted the Lord and also met some kids from our church. Don asked me if I would be willing to pick Fred up and bring him to church. Of course I agreed. So all of April and May we took him to church every Sunday mornng, went to the beach for lunch and returned in time for the evening service.

Around the end of May I got a horrendous phone call; Fred's mother was on the telephone, yelling and screaming at me. She was missing her diamond rings and wanted me to tell her that Fred wasn't with us Sunday afternoon—that was when she figured out that the rings were missing.

"But Fred was with us," I said.

She put the phone down and went to beat up Fred; I could hear it. She came back to the phone, yelling and screaming again. I knew it was a bad situation, so I told her I was coming over to talk to Fred. Fred had called me, too, asking me to get him away from his mother.

I got him out of the house and brought him back to our place to bandage him up.

"Does your mother do this to you very often?" I asked. "Why in heaven's name do you let her do it? Don't you ever try to defend yourself?"

He looked at me and his eyes got big. "I wouldn't hit my mother," he said.

I knew then that this kid had to have something. I took him back home and later Diane and I talked together about him. I said, "Hon, what would happen if the Lord wanted us to take Fred?"

"Well, you'd better call up the pastor and talk to him," she said.

I did, but Pastor thought I better not get involved because this was a dangerous situation. We talked about all the possibilities of taking a kid like that in, about legal guardianship, foster home, adoption. Finally we just dropped the subject.

We moved into a new apartment that summer, right next to the church. I went to the church one day to use the phone, before our own phone was installed. There was Fred sitting in the church yard.

I found out that the previous night his mom and dad had kicked him out of the house and that he was living in a slummy place with an "uncle" who was actually a friend of his mother's.

I said, "Look, why don't you come over to our place? I'll call your mother now and tell her to meet us over at our apartment. Maybe you can stay at our place this weekend until things get better."

She came and we made an agreement: She was going to give us fifty dollars, he could stay for a week and then we could review the situation.

We thought we were being nice people—helping the kid out, helping his mother out. The next Saturday at six o'clock in the morning, we heard a knock on the front door. I answered it and there was one of Fred's brothers. "Mom wants to see Fred out in her car," he said.

I could hear a car revving up down in the parking lot. *What in the world?* I thought. I went down to the parking lot where Fred's mother was sitting, drunk, in her red Mustang. "I want to see Fred," she said.

"What's the matter?" I asked.

"I am going to take Fred and run this car over the cliff," she said.

"Come upstairs and let's talk about this," I said. She came into the apartment with me and opened her purse. I saw a bottle of whiskey and a gun. She pulled both of them out and pointed the gun at Fred.

"Let's have a moment of silent prayer," I said. "Shall we all bow our heads, please?" Then I told Diane to get Fred into the bedroom and have him lock the door. I went into the living room with his mother and talked and coaxed and prayed with her until finally she broke down. Everything seemed fine and she left.

Then Fred came out of his room. All the time he was in his room he hadn't said a word or made a sound. He told us she probably wouldn't have killed him, but she would have done "something bad."

Diane and I talked about Fred's situation, and decided we'd do everything we could to help the boy. We told Fred he could stay with us all summer, but in my mind I knew that unless things got better, I couldn't send the kid back home, ever.

We went out and bought furniture in a Salvation Army store. We got him a chest of drawers and a desk; one of our friends loaned us a bed.

We didn't know that Fred had three brothers by his mother's first marriage and two brothers and a sister by his mother's second marriage. But by Monday, two of those brothers were also living with us.

Diane and I went into the bedroom and prayed, "Lord, we're not smart enough to know who to kick out and who to let stay. Please don't let anybody come here that's not supposed to be here. And don't let anybody stay here longer than they are supposed to."

Little did we know that that prayer would set the pattern for our lives for years to come!

I was getting about $200 a month from Ike, and Diane was getting about $350 from her secretary's job. All our bills came to just about $500, and we had three teen-age mouths to feed. Fred had turned thirteen at the end of July. I very quickly learned things about feeding boys. For instance, if you chop up tomatoes in an omelet, and you have only four eggs to go around for five people, the tomato makes the omelet squishy and no one will eat it.

At the end of August, we were really squeezing pennies. I came home late one night and impulsively said, "I think I'll make us a coffee cake." I baked a coffee cake with the last bit of Bisquick we had, and put it out for the four of us—Malcolm, Terry, Fred and I.

"Let's open a can of Vienna sausage," I said, and looked in the cupboard. There was one can left. This was Monday night and we weren't going to get paid until Friday.

I put the sausage on the plate and said, "Before we pray I need to get the ketchup." When I looked up from my prayer, there wasn't a single sausage on the plate.

"What happened to the sausage?" I asked.

The boys started to laugh. While I was getting the ketchup they thought they would play a joke on me so they ate all the sausage. They didn't know it was the last can.

"Boys, that was our last can of Vienna sausage for this whole week," I said.

They felt badly then and didn't even want to eat the coffee cake. What had started to be a time of sharing and fun together had turned out to be a bummer. Everybody got up quietly and went to bed.

I felt terrible, so I went to our bedroom and started to pray: "Lord, this is just awful. I don't think it's so bad to run out of food, that happens to everybody, but in front of these boys. We never asked for these boys."

I've learned it's better to tell the Lord what you feel because He knows how you feel anyway. There's no sense putting up a front on the outside when there's garbage on the inside.

I could have been making thousands of dollars a month. This wasn't the way it should be. We were supposed to be a testimony to these boys. And here we were—Diane and Mark Yasuhara; I was a Metropolitan

Opera winner, graduate of the University of Hawaii, sewing leis down in Waikiki for $200 a month. And we had run out of Vienna sausage. It wouldn't have been so bad if we had run out of steak, or even hamburger, but Vienna sausage—it cost forty-nine cents a can and we couldn't afford another one.

"Lord, please," I prayed, "please, not for our sakes, Diane's and mine, if You want to teach us some lesson on faith and You want us to go on a starvation diet, we can live on paper and water if You want us to. We will do that for You. But the boys don't know You that well and don't know this is a lesson of faith. So for their sakes, provide for them. Amen."

I went out to the boys, who weren't sleeping yet, and told them that God was going to provide within twenty-four hours, It wasn't so much faith as it was a lot of nerve. I went to bed.

We hadn't heard from Fred's mother for over a month and didn't even know where she was—she was going to give us fifty dollars, remember? Next morning we heard a knock on the door at about six or seven o'clock. There was Fred's mother, "dressed to the teeth."

She blew into the room and said, "I was just over to Las Vegas and was real lucky so I thought I would stop by and give you some money." She wrote out a check for $150.

How God answered prayer really made an impression on the boys. And there was a run on Vienna sausage at the market that week!

Fred came to us in the summer between his seventh and eighth grades in school. By that time, he had had two torrid love affairs. He had gone to his first drinking party when he was in the sixth. When he came to us he could hold his liquor quite well and was smoking a pack of cigarettes a day.

Fred was a sweet kid, but he was also a terror. I asked him one day, "Fred, do you have to smoke?"

He looked me straight in the eyes and said, "No!"

"Fred, this house is run on love and trust," I said. "We have you here because we love you and trust you. You can't really love someone if you don't trust them. If you have to smoke, tell me and we'll figure out times of the day when you can. But if you don't have to smoke, I wish you wouldn't."

He answered again, "No, no, no, I don't have to smoke."

"Okay, then we can make an agreement that you won't smoke from now on," I said. "I don't want you sneaking behind my back. If you feel you have to, just come to me and let me know."

"Sure, sure," he said.

Two weeks went by and he'd come home smelling like cigarette smoke. I'd say, "Fred, have you been smoking?"

"Oh, no, that's the cigarette smoke from the bus. The other kids are smoking," he answered.

He would come home from bowling and I would ask him the same question. The answer would be, "It's the smoke from the bowling alley."

One day I happened to be at the supermarket, which was on the other side of the bowling alley, at about four o'clock. I saw Fred standing there, smoking. When he saw me he smashed the cigarette in his hand.

I asked him to come straight home. I was furious. I wasn't so angry because he was smoking; I was angry because he had kept insisting he wasn't smoking, when all the time he had been.

I sat him down and said, "Freddie, I will never believe you again. We had an agreement that you weren't supposed to smoke. If you can't level with me on things like this, how are you going to level with me about things that I insist you do or don't do? I will never ever believe you again or trust you. That's it! You've had it. If you told me the sky was blue or purple or green or orange, I wouldn't believe you. If you told me it was raining, I wouldn't believe you unless I went out and checked myself."

Fred cried, "Oh, please, I'm really sorry."

"Well, sorry doesn't heal," I said. "Sorry doesn't change it. I forgive you, but I can't believe you anymore."

Then Fred went to his room. The Lord tapped me on the shoulder and said, "Mark, if I was that way with you, you would have been long gone."

I called Fred out of his room, and told him we would try again. I gave him a big hug.

That was another installment in my theology. It was only after this incident that I discovered the Living Bible's version of I Corinthians 13:7 which says, "If you love someone . . . you will always expect the best of him, always stand your ground in defending him." That's the way God is with us. No matter how "junky" we are, no matter how many times we do things behind His back, He still loves and forgives us. He made us basically to be good, so He knows our potential.

We planned to spend our first Christmas together with my folks in Hilo on the big island of Hawaii. We were to leave Honolulu on Christmas Day.

At about three o'clock on Christmas morning, we were suddenly awakened by two things: a sharp rapping on the door outside, and Fred shaking us and whispering fearfully, "My mother's outside. My mother's outside. I can see her through the screen door."

Oh, no, I thought, *what now?*

Then I had a brilliant idea: Diane, being a business

secretary, never seemed to have any problem dealing with these situations—especially when it came to other women. I sent her to the door while Fred and I huddled, scared stiff, under the blankets.

At the door Diane found Fred's mother and his stepfather with a box of food—a turkey, a ham and a lot of other goodies—and wanting to come in to wish us all a Merry Christmas.

But Diane, bless her heart, put on an air of cool indifference and thanked them for the gifts, adding that it was much too late for visiting, especially considering our flight to Hilo that morning—and simply closed the door.

That was that, except that Diane has never really let Fred and me live that night down.

When Fred had started to school in September, we realized that we needed some legal protection. I called a lawyer and he suggested that we file for either legal guardianship or adoption. But we would need consent of his parents. I asked Fred about adoption and he said no; he wanted to keep his last name because he wanted to be the only Valenzona who would make good in school. So we were going to file for guardianship. We started the process, but by Christmas the papers still hadn't come through.

On New Year's Eve in Hawaii, everybody buys strings of firecrackers and the entire island booms and cracks with the explosions of fireworks.

On our way to town to get fireworks, Fred sat in the car next to me. "Hey, can I change my name?" he asked suddenly.

I thought this was some kind of New Year's resolution. His given name was Freddie Lynn, a real winner.

"Sure, what name do you want?" I said jokingly.

"Your name," he said.

"Well, I have three names," I said. "Which one do you want?"

"Your last name."

It surprised me so that I pulled the car over to the side of the road and said, "Fred, what are you trying to say?"

"I want you to be my daddy and Diane to be my mommy," he said.

It was kind of like being proposed to. Of course, all of our friends weren't convinced that this was the best thing to do.

When we got back to Honolulu we called the lawyer and said we were going to file for adoption.

Soon after this, on a Sunday morning, we went through one of the many hassles parents have with their kids. I was twenty-three at the time, Diane was twenty-two, and Fred was thirteen.

I came home from church and went out to the back steps of the apartment. "Lord, I just cannot be a father to Fred," I said. "I don't have the look of a father, I don't have the dignity, the serenity, the wisdom—anything. I should be twice as old as I am. I just can't do it. What am I going to do, send him away?"

"Mark, I never asked you to be his father," the Lord said. "I am his father. I will be his father, his mother, his sister and his brother."

"Well, Lord, where do I come in?" I asked.

He said, "I have chosen to do My greatest work among men through men. So through you and Diane, I will be Fred's mother, father, sister and brother."

One night after a particularly discouraging day, I went into Fred's room and looked out the window at the mountains. The moon was just coming out from behind the clouds and I started to cry, "Lord, if I only had a mango tree . . . . If somebody could tell me how to do these things. If only I had my grandmother."

My Hawaiian grandmother was a great fat sweet lady. She had hardly any money, maybe five dollars spending money in a whole year. And with that five dollars she'd buy gum for us, stretching out the money over the entire year. I never heard my grandmother say a cross word. If we did something wrong, she'd never tell my mother; she knew we'd get a spanking.

We called her "Mama." If I was hurt, I ran to Mama. She would take me up into her lap and I would kind of go *swishhhh* down into all those folds of fat. She would rock me back and forth and sing songs such as "Jesu no ke kahu hipa"—"Savior, like a shepherd lead us, much we need Thy tender care." While I was standing there, looking out at the mountains wishing I was far away, somewhere else, that I was a little boy with my grandmother, I said, "Lord, if only You could be like my grandmother to me. If only I could feel Your big arms around me. Not just think it, but really feel it."

Suddenly I actually felt God's arms around me, as though He was picking me up and putting me on His lap and holding me close to Him. And He sang in my ear, "Savior, like a shepherd lead us, much we need Thy tender care," just as my grandmother had.

In August 1969, Diane and I became the parents of a thirteen-year-old son. His birth certificate now reads: "Father: Edward Mark Yasuhara, age 10; Mother: Diane Kunie Nishimoto, age 9."

We'll let Fred tell you his story in his own words.

8

Our Son Fred

My mother has been married four times as far as I know. She had three sons by her first husband and four more kids by her second one. I was the second to the oldest in the last batch.

When I was about five years old, my parents were having a lot of problems, mostly because of alcohol. They finally couldn't take it any more so they got a divorce. My father didn't want any of us, and my mother couldn't handle us so she left us with my grandmother in Hondeller. Mom took a job on the island of Kauai to start her life over again.

During this entire time my father never visited us; he just disowned all of us.

My mom came back one day and without notifying my grandmother, came to school and took me out of class. "We're going to see your daddy," she told me. Of course I was too young at the time to realize what was going on and was excited because I would get an airplane ride. She didn't take any of the other children.

When my brothers came to my class after school to pick me up, the teacher told them my mother had taken me to another island.

When they got home my grandmother said, "Where's Fred?" They just stood there and cried.

Then she shouted, "Where's Fred?!"

Then they told her, through their tears, "Fred is gone, Grandma. Fred is gone."

She got upset and called my real father. He told her that since my mother wanted me and since grandma didn't have legal custody over me, it would have to remain as it was.

During the entire flight mom tried to convince me that the man I was going to meet was my real father, though I was old enough to realize who my real father was. But I didn't care, I just ate it up. At least I would have a father.

So it was just the three of us. My new father owned a bar that had more business than most of the others on the island, so he was pretty well-to-do. This was to mom's advantage—she got all the money she wanted plus all the liquor she wanted. I guess that's why she went for him.

The eight years that I lived with them were the worst years of my life. My mother had always had an alcohol problem and was always drinking, losing her temper and getting drunk. But when she wasn't drinking, she was the best lady in the world, really a beautiful person. But those times were rare; most of the time she was drunk and fighting with my stepfather.

Our apartment was in the back of the bar, so I rarely saw them because they got up early in the morning to clean. The bar was open from late morning through midnight and into the next morning. During the summer I usually hung around the bar and watched the goings-on.

Sometimes, late at night, especially when my parents fought, my mother took me out of bed and said, "Come on, you are coming with me." She raised me in such fear of her that I did anything she said so I wouldn't get a beating or some other punishment. She got me dressed and then would take me bar-hopping practically all night long. I had to listen to her yell, scream, laugh and drink. If I tried to say that I was tired or sleepy, she would slap me or even take me outside and beat me.

I couldn't say anything about her treatment of me to anyone because I knew she would get back at me. For instance, I have two scars that I know are the result of some of the tortures I received. I forget the reason, but once she told me to stick out my hand; then she pressed her burning cigarette to it. I got upset by that so I told my stepfather; she came back and burned my leg in the same way she had burned my hand.

It was terrible and all along I was really scared of her. If she told me to do something and I didn't get up and do it right then, she would hit me and say I was slow, and call me all sorts of names. She really had a problem and was messed up, I think, in her head.

One time she took me to a friend's house and took along a six-pack of beer, which she made me carry. She sat me down in the living room and gave me a bottle of beer while she was in the kitchen drinking. So she started me off drinking when I was only eight years old.

Later during that same year she started me smoking; she gave me some cigarettes and showed me how to do it. In a sense I knew it was wrong. I thank God I didn't get to the place where I was hooked. Now as I look back, I realize that the Lord had His hand on my life.

The best thing about the whole deal was that right after I finished fourth grade, Billy Graham came to the Islands. I used to spend my spare time at the movies. It just so happened that one theater was running one of his movies. Mr. Graham was there and was going to speak.

I saw the movie and it really didn't make much sense to me because I was too young to understand it at the time. But I remembered what Mr. Graham had to say. It was about having a friend and how Jesus Christ could be a close friend of mine—someone to whom I could come.

This appealed to me because I really didn't have anyone close to me. A lot of people were my friends because we had money and they knew it.

When Mr. Graham gave the invitation, I went forward and gave my heart to the Lord. I didn't have anyone to help me in the things of God, so I didn't learn any more about Jesus.

When I was about twelve, my stepfather sat me down and told me that he had stayed with my mother as long as he had because he wanted to wait until I was old enough to make a decision on my own. Now he was going to get a divorce. So when it came time to say who I wanted to live with, I had to choose mom because I was so afraid of her and I knew she would hurt me.

Of course my stepfather understood this so I went to live with my mother.

One Sunday my mother came to me and said she had to leave for the big island of Hawaii and take care of some business in Kailua Kona, which is a little town on the island. She said she would probably be there for a day or two and would be back, at the latest, on Wednesday.

"I'm going to leave you here and the boy next door is going to take you to school. I have already talked to him," she told me.

I replied, "Sure, that's fine." I thought it was good because I had a telephone in the apartment, beer in the icebox, and all the cigarettes I wanted—everything couldn't be better.

But soon I got lonesome and was unhappy because two and a half weeks later she had still not come home. I hadn't heard a word from her and she left me no money. Fortunately, my stepfather stopped by while I was in school and left some food and money on the table for me. Once in a while he came to sit and talk with me or he took me out to play ball. One day he realized that my mom had never returned.

He called my mother's lawyer who was on Oahu and explained to him the situation. So he called my aunt, mom's sister, and told her to come and get me until they could figure out what to do with me. She came, took me out of school, and said, "Pack your bags, we are going to my home in Honolulu."

"Well, what about mom? Where is she?" I asked. I was afraid that something had happened.

My aunt said, "We can't get hold of her anyway. There is no way we can contact her so we are just going to have to leave a note here for her whenever she comes back, because we don't know whether she is dead or alive. We just don't know where she is."

I was kind of glad to get away from there.

My brothers and grandparents lived on Oahu, so I got to see my family again after eight years.

My older brother, Terrence, and I were together a lot. He was rather wild, so that was the wrong thing for me. I was always getting into trouble in school, but the vice-principal of the school, Dan Haas, was a Christian and the Lord had impressed upon his heart to pray for me.

Of course, I didn't find this out until later. He had noticed that I really needed a friend, so he tried to make friends with me. Being the type of person I was, I didn't go for that.

But he kept calling me to his office and talking to me. (Several times he had to back up his talks with the board of education to my back end!) After awhile I got used to the fact that people knew I was friends with the vice-principal. I have gone in to him and told him a little more about my life than he could see through the records.

He invited me to go to a Christian camp, saying that he would sponsor me. I kept saying that I didn't want to go. What would I do at a Christian camp? I was just too big of a person—I wouldn't lower myself to do something like that.

He kept asking me, "Do you want to go?"

I kept saying, "No, I don't want to go."

One day when I came home to my aunt's house, I saw my mom standing at the top of the stairs. I hadn't seen her for months. I broke out in a cold sweat because I was scared she was going to tear me up because I had left. I couldn't avoid her so I walked straight up to her. She opened her arms with a big smile on her face and hugged me. I could smell the liquor all over her, but she acted really nice and sweet.

Of course, nothing had happened so she still had legal control over me. She said, "Come on, you are going with me."

I had no choice. I went with her to live in a house which was about seven blocks away. During the time she had been gone—a total of three months—she had married a man who was a war veteran and who had a lot of money coming in from the war-social security and from other sources. He also was an alcoholic, so they had at least something in common. By this time she was really bad off. She had put a lot of weight on; her face was all swollen. She looked terrible. It really hurt me inside, and of course this made me even more upset about the whole thing.

In the meantime I had been taking karate lessons. I had thought to myself one day, "If she slaps me around, I'll protect myself." But then I thought again, "Well, I better not because she might get mad and do something drastic."

I had informed Mr. Haas of all this and he was praying for me. Soon the camp date came up, and still I didn't want to go. I was home alone, doing nothing, and all of sudden I thought, "Well, I think I'll go to that camp." I picked up the phone and told Mr. Haas that I had decided to go to the camp. That was a breakthrough, because this was humbling myself and stepping into territory I knew very little about.

Mr. Haas kind of laughed and said, "Well, I knew that the Lord would work everything out."

So the next day I got ready and went off to camp. Right before we left for camp a little sports car drove up and Mr. Haas said, "Oh, here are some friends of mine from the Kalihi Union Church. They're choir leaders of the church and I'd like you to meet them."

He introduced me to Mark and Diane Yasuhara. I said, "Hi," and made small talk. He told me a little bit about them and then I got on the bus and took off for this Christian camp.

I was very cold and unfriendly because these were Christian kids, and I didn't feel like I belonged. I was really uptight. But all the way to the camp, these kids were friendly to me. They asked me all kinds of questions. I thought, *Are they trying to get something out of me? What's their angle?* I just couldn't figure it out. I started to get upset, but the more upset I got the more pleasant they were. It really tore me up inside.

I couldn't figure out what in the world was going on. Then I started hearing all kinds of things about Jesus and about having peace.

Finally it all came together. I had been wondering, *What's with these kids—are they crazy or something? Are they putting me on and acting like they are happy?* It was too much for me. Then it hit me—they were doing this and behaving this way because they really had this peace in their lives. As messed up as I was, I wanted it, but I didn't know how to say it. I wanted to be happy.

On the last day of camp we were sitting around the campfire. The leader asked us to stand up and share what the Lord had done for us at camp. The kids, one after another, got up and shared. I listened to other people share what the Lord had done for them. It was really getting to me inside—my mind and heart rattled on and on.

I started thinking, *Well, maybe I ought to get up and tell them what I think about them.* Then I thought, *No.* This went on forever in my mind, or it seemed so. Finally I couldn't stand it any longer. I just had to get it out of me. I got the worst case of stage fright I ever had; I was scared. I didn't know what to do or say. It broke me and I started to cry; I told them I wanted to accept Jesus.

They prayed for me and for the first time in my life I knew on the inside that I was a Christian because I had peace. At the time of the Billy Graham Crusade, I didn't really know what was going on. Now, after all the tears and praying, all I said was, "Well, I guess I should go to church."

I was extremely ignorant about everything. The kids talked to me about things I should do and most of them volunteered to help me. I felt good inside; I was able to smile and to really love people. I realized that this had been my longing. I wanted to love and all this time I hadn't known how. I never knew what love was until I met the Lord.

For some reason I decided to go to Kalihi Union Church. I had friends there, but most of my friends went to Makiki Christian, and so did Don Haas. He explained to me that the friends whom I had met before I left for camp, Mark and Diane, lived only a couple of blocks from me and that they would pick me up and take me to church.

When we got back from camp, Mark was there at the church to pick me up. He wanted to take me home so he could find out where I lived. On the way, he stopped to pick up Diane from work. They took me to my house and we set up the time and place where he could pick me up for church. I got to know them pretty well. They treated me like a little brother.

I was still living with my mom, and one day she and I got into a fight. She started kicking me and throwing bottles at me. I put my foot down and thought, *Well, I'll just block and try to protect myself.* She grabbed my hair and started beating on me. My face got all cut up. Finally she threw me down on the floor and went to her bedroom. I called Mark and asked him to pick me up because I didn't want to stay with my mother another minute.

Soon Mark pulled up and I ran outside the house and got in his car. He took me to his apartment, and he and Diane talked with me about what had happened. Mark tried his best to patch me up. They prayed that the Lord would help my mother and protect me from her. Later on I went back home. The following day mom got mad because I had called Mark and told him about her beating me. She started beating me again.

This time I blocked her and as she kicked me she fell and hit her head against the wall. This really "teed her off." She hollered at her husband, "Where's my gun? Where's my gun?"

He told her it was in the closet. She turned and went into her bedroom. I saw her pull the pistol down out of the closet. I thought I'd better leave.

I got out of the house and ran up the street several blocks to my aunt's house. She had said that if I ever needed to run away I could come to her and she would take care of me. I told her about the fight and she thought she should call the police. So they called the police and the police—for protection reasons—put me in a detention home. I went in on Wednesday and was supposed to get out on Friday. But my social worker was sick, so I was in the home from Wednesday through the next Monday.

During this time, the police and some other people were able to talk to my mom and dad to see what they could work out as far as placing me in another home. Mom didn't want me to go, so they gave up.

Monday came and the officer took me out of the room and said that I had a visitor, and that my social worker, the officer, my mom and I would sit down and talk things over. Mom was sober so she was really nice and she apologized to me. The social worker asked her if she would ever assault me again. In the meantime the police had taken the gun away from her and had discovered that it wasn't registered. She promised me that things like this would never happen again.

I wanted to get out of the detention home because the kids in it were really bad. I thought that going with my mother was a way out.

She was nice to me after we got home. The next day, however, she was drunk again. We were all sitting there watching TV and all of a sudden my mother's husband said, "I don't like him. I want him out."

So I said, "Okay, I'll leave."

"No," my mom said.

"Either you or him," my mother's husband said.

"I'll leave then," I said. I got up, took some clothes, and went over to the church. I sat on the front lawn and cried because I knew I didn't have a home.

All of a sudden a truck came driving up. Mark and a student of his were in it. Mark said, "Hi. You want to help me move? I'm moving into an apartment right down here a couple of blocks from the church and I need some help."

"Sure," I said.

So he loaded some furniture, which he had stored at church, onto his truck and they took off.

About an hour later he came back to the church by himself.

"What's wrong?" he asked. "How come you're sitting here by yourself?"

"I'm just sitting here thinking," I said.

"You look awfully disturbed. Is something wrong?" he asked. "I thought you were coming down to help me. What's the matter?"

"Oh, I don't know," I said.

He knew I had a five o'clock curfew so I could report to my mother. It was getting close to five and he said, "Well, you better come down and help me pretty soon because soon it will be five and you have to go home."

"No, I don't," I said.

"Sure, sure," Mark said.

"Well, I don't have a home to go to anymore," I quickly answered.

He looked at me, then realized that I wasn't kidding. "Well, why don't you come down to the apartment and we'll talk about it."

I went with him and explained to him what had happened.

"Well, why don't you just stay here tonight and we will try to work something out," he said.

The next day he told me, "We decided that Diane will talk to your mother and see if she will let you stay here."

In the meantime my mother had arranged for me to stay with a friend of hers who lived in a studio apartment in back of someone's house. The apartment was rat and roach infested and didn't have any toilets; I would have to go to another house to use the bathroom. Mark said that he didn't think that would be too good and that I would be welcome to stay in their apartment. I told mom about it and she said that would be fine.

One day Mark said to me, "You are going to have to start to school again so we better get some kind of legal guardianship for you, so your mom can't just come and take you away."

I said, "Okay." But they asked my mom and she wouldn't sign any release.

Then we went through a lot of hassles trying to get her to sign. Finally we got her signature and Mark and Diane became my legal guardians.

The day I moved in with them was three days before my thirteenth birthday. Mark and Diane had a surprise birthday party for me. That was the first real birthday party I ever had.

Mark took me out that morning saying we were going to go for a ride to the shopping center and look around. We got to the shopping center and he let me go shopping. I bought a lot of neat clothes—I didn't have many. Then he took me to a photographer and had some pictures taken; he had a couple of them done in oil.

Finally, we got back to the apartment. As I walked in the door, a bunch of streamers hit my face and a big group of kids from the church hollered, "Surprise!"

I was thrilled. I had just moved in with Mark and Diane and couldn't figure out how anyone could be so generous.

Sometime after my thirteenth birthday, Mark and I were talking and he asked me if I wanted to be adopted. He said that he and Diane had been talking and they thought that adoption would work out great. We had grown close. I loved them and they loved me.

I didn't go for this adoption bit, though, because in the meantime I had been playing baseball. My brother and I had made a name for ourselves as a pitcher and catcher duo in baseball and we were taking care of almost the whole conference. I didn't want to give up my last name for that reason. All I thought about was myself, so I said no.

It was a mistake to say no, because I really cared for them. I felt that they were my own parents and I wanted to start over, get rid of my old name, and be a new person completely.

At Christmas we went to the big island to visit Mark's folks. We were on our way to town to buy some fireworks for New Year's and I felt that this was the perfect time to talk to Mark. So I said, "Mark, I want to change my name to your name."

Kiddingly he said, "Which name do you want—I've got three names."

"No, I'm serious," I said.

He pulled over to the side of the road and we talked. It was beautiful—we prayed about it and went on.

As soon as we got back to Honolulu we started arranging the adoption with the lawyer.

From then on, I called Mark and Diane "dad" and "mom." It wasn't hard for me at all. It seemed so natural. All this time they had been calling me their little brother. "Little brother" in Hawaiian is *kuukaina*. When they started the adoption, they said, "We'll have to change your name around a little bit."

Originally my name was Freddie Lynn Valenzona. We had to have my name changed since I was being adopted. I suggested that I have the Yasuhara name and just get rid of Valenzona. So they decided that my name would be changed from Freddie to Frederic. My middle name was Lynn and I didn't want that, so Mark decided to name me after him. He and Diane both thought that they ought to give me a Hawaiian name. So they went to a friend of theirs who was a Hawaiian lady, and she gave me a Hawaiian name. My Hawaiian name is Ikaikikuukainaokamanaokealoha, which means "my courageous little brother in the spiritual strength of love." So my full name is now Frederic Mark Ikaikikuukainaokamanaokealoha Yasuhara.

I started back to school and everybody knew there was something different about me. It was really hard for me to share with them the change in my life because before I had been such a bully.

The first part of my eighth grade year didn't turn out so well because everybody seemed turned against me and grade-wise I was terrible. Mark and Diane sat me down and said, "Listen, we will just have to do something about your grades because you can't get out of eighth grade with F's."

So with the Lord's help and mom and dad's we got together and prayed about my problems. I put my foot down and really started thinking about my grades. I just trusted the Lord that everything would work out. I got out of eighth grade with a C average which was pretty good after getting F's and D's.

That summer we left for the mainland. This was when dad won the San Francisco Opera contest.

My first year on the mainland was spent at Staunton, Virginia, and I started school at Wilson Memorial High School. This was perfect for me because I was in a new area and felt like a brand-new person, a brand-new Christian, and I could start a new life.

I started just being a completely different person—out-going and friendly like I had always wanted to be. The Lord really blessed me with all kinds of honors and awards. I wasn't in school three weeks before I was nominated and voted to be the homecoming escort for the freshman class. This was exciting for me because I was chosen out of 2,300 kids.

During this time, mom and dad were traveling in their concert ministry which was just beginning. I stayed with the Knopps who had a family of nine boys—some really beautiful Christian people. The Lord blessed me with things like becoming drum major of the band. My grades went up to B's, which was really exciting for me. I also was elected to the student council.

Finally the first semester ended and dad decided that we would move to Kansas City, and they said they would take care of me. I packed up quickly and flew to Kansas City—I had short notice. I stayed with Bruce and Becky Rowe the last half of my sophomore year.

When I got to Park Hill I got into all kinds of things that really excited me. The Lord blessed me in these things which made in an impression on some of the other kids, which in turn opened doors for me to witness.

After several more moves, I started my senior year at Olathe High School. I started off as student council president. The Lord has blessed me ever since I have given my life to Him.

Since I gave my life to the Lord, everything has been a constant gradual step up, growing, learning, and experiencing things. All through this time I still have the hangups of my temper and a few other things. But with the Lord's help, I will be able to overcome these. I praise and thank the Lord for my parents, Mark and Diane, who have taught me and brought me through a lot.

As I look back, I can't imagine or can't even start to count all the things and all the blessings that the Lord has given me. I just can't see how someone as great as God can care for someone as small as I.

9

Waiting, Waiting

In January 1969, Ike invited me to the Phoenix regional convention of the Full Gospel Businessmen's Fellowship International. I was not scheduled as a soloist but Ike, in his winning way, got a spot for me to sing the first night. As a result, they asked me to sing as many times as I could during the convention. It was the first big break I had.

It was the last afternoon of the convention and I had just sung. Demos Shakarian got up and said, "Mark, do you have a record, an album that people can take home?"

"Sorry, I don't," I said.

"How many of you would like Mark to make an album?" he asked.

It seemed like hundreds raised their hands. "Would you people please stand up?" Demos asked. "Now would each of you put down five dollars as the payment for Mark's first album and then we will send it to you when it is made."

How I praise the Lord for the faith of Demos Shakarian. Before the service was over, Norvel Hayes came up to Demos and said he would produce the album.

So instead of going back to Hawaii, I flew out to Tennessee and then down to Atlanta, Georgia, to record my first album which was titled *Beyond the Sky*. We did the entire album in six hours. I had just met the organist and the pianist that morning, and we learned, rehearsed and recorded twelve songs in that short six hours. (That was during my younger years when I could sing for six hours straight.)

I flew back home and said, "Praise God, the doors have been opened." I had all kinds of exciting visions.

We waited for months—and nothing.

The only door that opened up for us was the door to the apartment. Open the door, go to work; come home, open the door, shake out the rug; open the door, come back in the house; open the door, sit on the steps and cry. Day after day just sitting there, waiting for the phone call that never came. I didn't know what to do, so I decided to get depressed. Every month we were just making it financially. I knew that we could be doing much better if I had taken the school job or if I were entertaining down on Waikiki.

Many of my good Christian friends would ask, "Mark, what are you doing now?"

"Nothing much," I'd say. "Just waiting on the Lord."

"Well, aren't you helping Ike?"

"No, I don't have to go down to the shop anymore."

"Aren't you working?" they would ask.

"No, I'm just waiting for the Lord," I said. I could feel them thinking, *If Mark were a responsible husband, he would get a job. And they have this kid living with them too I understand. Not very wise, if you ask me.*

At the end of March we had another typical family hassle, it was the straw that broke the camel's back. I took the car out at about eleven o'clock at night and began to drive. I drove and drove and cried and cried. I had no idea that a year later we would be involved full-time in a ministry. All I knew was that for nine months I had been waiting around and nothing had happened. If you are on the mainland, you can at least move to another state. In Hawaii, you're stuck! I had turned down several jobs and that in a tight job market. It was depressing, and people were saying I was just lazy.

After driving for a long time, I found myself on the other side of the island of Oahu at the edge of a cliff; the waves were crashing on the jagged rocks below. Don't ask me how I knew where that place was, but that's where I ended up. Nobody for miles around. Only those huge waves crashing up on this cliff in the dark night. I drove to the edge and something told me to drive the car over the cliff. *Fasten your seat belt, roll down the window and forget about the whole big mess. You've followed Jesus and look where it's gotten you. You've been duped. Brainwashed. You've missed the boat. You aren't spiritual enough to handle it. You can't even do things everybody else does naturally. What makes you think you're going to excell in a ministry? Where are all your friends? What's happened to all your investments of time, energy, emotions, love, and money?*

I sat in the car for hours, crying, trying to get up enough nerve to drive over the edge of the cliff.

Being the Hawaiian that I am, I fell asleep. When I woke up, it was eleven-thirty in the morning. The Hawaiian sun was shining in a sky filled with beautiful white clouds. The ocean was beautiful. And I was starved.

I went to a local greasy spoon and got a hamburger. About five minutes after I ate the hamburger, I began feeling sick. What does a kid do when he gets sick? He goes home. I forgot all about the melodrama of the night before and headed for home.

It was a good four-hour drive home. On the way, I had to stop by the side of the road by a bush to throw up. It was as if a lot of evil I had been harboring inside came out. I had been blaming my parents, my church, and everybody else for where I was now. If I wasn't so Christian, we wouldn't be going through these hassles. If we didn't have Fred; if we weren't so narrow-minded and dedicated we wouldn't be in such a financial mess. . . .

By the time I got home they were ready to call the police. I grew a notch during those twenty-four hours, and that day I experienced real deliverance in my life.

All during April a woman kept calling me and asking that I compete in the San Francisco Opera auditions. I said I didn't want to have anything to do with opera.

"But we need you," she said. "As a Metropolitan Opera winner, you would add so much to the competition."

I found out that the second prize was $300—we owed that much in taxes—so I said I'd enter.

The contest was held in the middle of May and I won first prize: $500 with an all-expenses-paid round trip to San Francisco for the finals and eight weeks of training in the Merola Opera School.

Norvel Hayes had told me to let him know if I was ever on the mainland, and he would fly me to Tennessee from wherever I was so I could do some concerts. I called Norvel and said, "I'm going to be in San Francisco during June. Would you like me to come to Tennessee?"

"Oh, yes," Norvel said.

I spent a month there giving seven concerts a week. It was great to be working and used of the Lord.

When I had been in Phoenix in January, the FGBFI men had invited me to their international convention in

Washington, D.C. While I was with Norvel, I said, "Norvel, we cannot go unless they take care of our expenses." He called the California office and we got the promise, "Yes, we will take care of both Mark and Diane's expenses to and from Hawaii. Tell them to come on and we'll take care of them."

I figured out with Diane how she and Fred could come to San Francisco for the summer and then the three of us could fly to Washington, D.C. in July. We had enough money for three one-way tickets to Washington.

I went to the San Francisco Opera auditions at the end of June and did well. I didn't win, but the judges seemed to be impressed.

As part of the Merole program I was to do the tenor lead in Verdi's *Rigoletto*. I asked to be excused during the first week of the school so we could fly to the FGBFI convention in Washington, which was to be held the first part of July.

We missed our plane so I went to school. That day one of the associate directors said that there is much competition and few people make a decent living out of opera. Those who want to do well have to sell out completely to opera: it has to mean more than their families, more than anything else in the world. It was almost an evangelistic appeal.

Well, I thought, *he's too late because I've already sold out to Jesus. I can't do this.* On the plane to Washington, I said, "Lord, I don't want to go back there. I know I am not going to be successful in opera—not if that is what I'd have to do." I realize now that man was talking about values and priorities, and that had the Lord planned for me to do the opera scene, I would have been successful, happy and fulfilled. The fact that there are opera stars today who are committed Christians proves that. But evidently God didn't have the opera world in His plans for me.

We were all primed for our first trip to Washington, D. C. Six thousand people at a world FGBFI convention and we were being flown in as guests. We dressed up in our Hawaiian regalia and walked into the breakfast meeting as the people were finishing the meal. We had come directly from the plane and had had about three hours of sleep. Fred wondered what we were going to do. I said, "Let's stand here at the back of the hall. Somebody will see us and call us up to the front."

We stood for an hour under the air conditioning vent. Nobody recognized us. A couple of people came up to us and said, "Oh, what country are you folks from?" I kind of got the picture that we were not only unrecognized but that we weren't even expected. Ike was at the breakfast; he finally saw us and took us to his table. That morning Ike was asked to share his testimony, so he called me up to sing. By this time the light had dawned—someone had made a mistake. We had found out during the time we were at the table that no one was expecting us, we weren't budgeted—and we had flown in with only twenty dollars in our pockets, figuring that all our expenses were being taken care of.

I was tired so I said, "Oh, Lord Jesus, what should I sing?" The only song that came to my mind was "Savior, Like a Shepherd Lead Us." That seemed to be really appropriate: "In Thy pleasant pastures feed us:" "For our use Thy folds prepare." Here we were checked into the Washington Hilton for four days and we had only twenty dollars and no credit cards. I sang it straight from the heart. People to this day tell us they remember that first song I sang in Washington.

"Look, Mark," Ike said, "the Lord will take care of everything. Just be at every service ready to sing—something is going to happen here."

At this particular convention, the meetings were planned very loosely. You just had to be on call. We went to every morning, afternoon, and evening service all dressed up ready to go on. We waited, waited, waited for three days. Friday afternoon Diane said, "Well, forget it. I am going to visit my relatives." Fred was out with the youth so I thought I'd better go to the service. It would be just our luck that the day we were not there was the day somebody would call on us. I went, but I didn't have a victorious spirit.

The man in charge of the meeting kept calling this quartet, but the quartet didn't show up. So he finally said, "Since the quartet isn't here, let's see, who else can we—hey, that brother from Hawaii, what's his name? Is he here—that brother from Hawaii who sang the other morning? We don't have the quartet; maybe he can give us a number."

Metropolitan Opera winner; San Francisco Opera winner; potentially one of the great young tenors in the world; rated as the most outstanding up and coming young music teachers in Hawaii. *We don't have our southern gospel quartet so we are going to ask him to sing, as a last resort.*

As I walked that long walk to the platform, the devil said to me, "You see, Mark, this is what happens when you start fooling around with these mickey mouse Christians. You'll always be inserted on the spur of the moment—no thought, no consideration, no nothing—just a filler. Do you want to be a filler all your life singing for the Lord?"

My head was so badly messed up that I couldn't think of a single song. But I thought of a key as I passed the pianist—the key of E flat. Between the piano and the rostrum I thought, *Now what song do I know in E flat?*

The only song I knew in that key was "Great Is Thy Faithfulness". That was the last song I wanted to sing then. But I sang it anyway, and cracked on the top note at the end. I thought, *This is the limit. I give up.* I went to my room, locked the door—Fred and Diane were out—and lay down on a bed and sobbed.

After I cleared myself a little, I said, "Lord, I can only figure that three things might have happened. First, we may have missed your will. Knowing the way I was raised up that is the most probable one. I don't think it's fair that a person will do all he can do to follow You only to suddenly find himself way out in the bushes. If I'm getting off the track, I think that you're the kind of God who loves me enough to let me know. Way down deep, I don't believe that You're like a lot of people think You are—that if a person really trusts You, nine times out of ten he ends up on the losing end unless he's super-spiritual."

I told the Lord that He knew better than anyone else that I wasn't that kind of person, and if that was the only kind of person who would ever make it, we could just forget, starting then.

"Or perhaps You want us to hitchhike home," I continued. "You are going to teach us some heavy lesson about roughing it across the mainland wilderness. If that's so, we will just have to take it on the chin.

"Maybe there's another possibility and that is that You are trying to tell us not to go back home but to stay here on the mainland for some kind of full-time ministry. If You are doing that, could You forego the still small voice? Right now, I need a booming, 'Mark, I want you to -- --' whatever it is You want us to do. If I write back to Hawaii and tell them that we decided to stay and they find out that we couldn't get back home anyway, they won't think that is the leading of God. They are just going to think that that is typical of Mark's scatterbrain—he just didn't plan ahead. Please make it very obvious, not only to us, but to the folks at home."

The next morning (the last day of the convention) we sang, "There's One above all other friends to me, His name is Jesus, and I love Him so. Take my reputation, take my dearest blood relation, just give me Jesus, for I love Him so."

While we were singing, people began to line up backstage to invite us to their cities and churches—and to give us money. We walked through the lobby after the morning session was over and people would stick money in our pockets and just walk away. Our pockets were bulging with dollar bills so we went to our room to empty our pockets. We went downstairs again and I said, "Now let's walk through the lobby again—real slow this time." As long as we were in the lobby people kept coming and stuffing our pockets with money.

By the end of the convention that night, we had over $400 in cash, and over 100 invitations to major cities in the United States. We figured that was a booming voice from God, and what He wanted us to do was obvious.

Our first invitation was to come to an Assemblies of God church the very next day, which was Sunday. On Monday we were driven down to Virginia where we were with Demos Shakarian at a banquet which the Shenandoah Valley chapter of the Full Gospel Businessmen Fellowship International was having for him.

At the end of the banquet, I was packing up my autoharp—you know how you have your head down when you are packing—and I saw several pairs of legs standing in front of me. I looked up and here were five good-looking young men with their mom and dad. I found out they were part of the Knopp family—there were nine boys in all.

"Do you folks live on a farm?" I asked.
"Not really," they said, "but we do have a few acres outside of Staunton."
"Do you have cows?"
"Yeah, we have a cow."
"It gives real milk?"
"Yeah."

Now we were never able to afford fresh milk when I was a kid and I thought having a cow in the Shenandoah Valley had to be almost next to heaven.

"Can we come over for lunch sometime?" I asked. "I'd really like to go to a place like that."

They thought it was a great idea, so in a few days we went over to the Knopp's place for lunch. This was the beginning of a beautiful relationship with the Knopp family. God taught us so many things through them. For two years their modest old farm house in Staunton, Virginia, was our home.

To many people, any boy is a potential terror—toads and snails and puppy dog tails and all that. Just the idea of *nine* boys . . . .

I'm sure Paul and Christine Knopp had their share of puppy dog tails and snails, and the boys tell us that they had their share of what somebody called "tough love" applied locally to their behinds. But when we came into the picture the Knopps were to us the visual expression of Forever Aloha. Six-year-old Danny was the youngest, and John and Joseph, twins and the eldest, were about twenty years old. Then there's David, Thomas and Timothy (a second set of twins), Mark, Stephen and Nathan. When we arrived at the house—an old farm house that has been under constant restoration since they first moved in—all nine boys ushered us through the back door, through the washroom, where "Mama"

Knopp grinds her own wheat and makes her own yogurt, and into the rustic Better-Homes-and-Garden kitchen.

(We didn't learn until later that except for one other evangelist and his family, the Knopps had never had company at all, mostly because Christine was embarrassed that the house wasn't "nice.")

We all sat down at the long wooden table; those who didn't sit on the bench sat on one of the motley assortment of chairs. Christine served up what has become a sentimental and palatable favorite of ours: old fashioned chicken and dumplings. There were piles of her fantastic whole wheat bread—course and thick—with lots of peanut butter and honey to go along with it.

But it was the salad that stole our hearts—or what was said about the salad dressing. We had shredded lettuce and kind of apologetically, Christine offered us two dressings, one which she had made and one which she had purchased from the store.

Well, coming from a poor family, who more often than not couldn't afford a lot of "store-bought" things, I was one of many American kids who assumed that if you could buy it, it was better.

Not so with the Knopps. Immediately after Christine said we could use the commercial dressing "if you'd rather," Stephen piped up with, "Mama got the store dressing because you're company, but we'd rather have hers any day!"

It was over that salad dressing that our love affair with this beautiful, gentle, deeply spiritual family began. I guess it was "love at first bite." We were there several weeks and in time it became our home.

One day, not too long after our first meeting, I noticed that I was always the only one taking seconds at dinner. I asked David, "How come you guys don't take seconds at the table?"

He hemmed and hawed around and finally admitted that since there was never enough food for everyone to have seconds, they wanted us to be the ones to have whatever seconds there were. I could hardly believe that these children could be so considerate and thoughtful.

Many times we have overheard Christine say, "Praise the Lord," and "Thank you, Jesus," in almost breathless wonder as she washed the endless number of pots and pans or folded the constant stack of towels and clothes. This serenity overflowed to the boys. Rarely have we heard either Paul or Christine shout—even to call the little boys in from play. To do that, Christine would simply tap on the kitchen window with a spoon. Where I came from, the kitchen windows would have broken if our mothers had tried getting our attention that way. But these boys had their ears tuned to that tapping.

Paul pastored a little white chapel, sitting picturesquely in a grove of oak trees a few miles from their house. For years, very few people attended until one Sunday when again only the eleven Knopps were present, Paul and Christine and the boys prayed together to see if the Lord might show them whether they should continue or join the fellowship of another church in town.

After they prayed, each of them, from the youngest to the oldest, opened his Bible and randomly let a finger fall on any Scripture. Danny read his first, then Nathan read his. . . . When Paul had finished reading his verse, they had heard eleven different verses instructing them to remain where they were.

Sometime later, they did the same thing, and they got eleven different verses saying once again that they were to stay in the ministry God had called them to.

Today they no longer meet in the little chapel. Instead, more than 100 people gather every Sunday in a large extended room at the Knopps' house for some of the most beautiful, spontaneous, Spirit-led worship, preaching and teaching we have ever been a part of.

We are no longer living with the Knopps, but many others have more than replaced us. Never do they have fewer than twenty people sit down at the table for supper. Since that first meal of chicken and dumplings and shredded lettuce, hundreds of people have experienced God's kind of serenity, togetherness, and Forever Aloha through the quiet, unassuming, living ministry of this family.

Realizing that the Lord wanted us to stay indefinitely on the mainland, we went back to Hawaii at the end of that summer to take care of our belongings. We already had a round-trip ticket to Hawaii from San Francisco, but the problem was that we had to get back to Roanoke, Virginia, where our first concert was scheduled.

We went back to Hawaii and I thought we could sell all our stuff, car and everything, to finance the trip to Virginia. The first night we were back home the car was stolen. The thief had run out of gas two blocks down the road, but he—or they—had jammed the gears and broken a little pin in the gears. The mechanic said it would take six months to get a new pin. So we couldn't sell the car. None of the other things sold for much money because we had to sell them in a hurry.

But the night we left, people came to the airport and gave us envelopes, some of them with gifts in them. In the airplane we praised the Lord as we opened the envelopes and found these expressions of our friends' love.

When we got to California, we made the arrangements to catch our flight to Virginia. We hadn't yet paid for the tickets, we just had reservations. Our plane from Hawaii was late so we missed the flight we were supposed to be on and the next flight wasn't going to leave for another nine hours.

When we got to the ticket counter, the ticket agent said,"That will be $372.22." We took out all the money we had been given, which we hadn't counted yet, and with all our nickels and dimes, we had exactly $375!

We had a nine-hour wait and about two dollars between the three of us. I remembered that we could get a refund for the meal we hadn't eaten on our flight from Hawaii. The meal was an optional ten dollars, which we had bought. But my mother had packed us a lunch, so we had told the stewardess we weren't going to eat the meal. She said we should mention this to the ticket agent to get a refund on three meals.

But for two and a half hours I went all over the Los Angeles airport trying to get a refund on those meals. Nobody would give me a refund until finally one agent said, "Let me see those tickets again . . . I'm sorry, sir, you can't get a refund for tickets that haven't been used."

"What do you mean?" I asked. I was tired, exasperated, and it was two-thirty in the morning.

"These tickets haven't been cancelled," he said. "They haven't even been used. When are you going to make the trip?"

"We just landed about three hours ago."

"I'm sorry," he said, "I don't know. It hasn't been torn yet."

"Oh, no. What am I going to do?" I asked.

"Well, I tell you what, I can give you a refund for the entire ticket."

"Don't do that," I said. "Just give us the money for the meals."

"I can't do that because I won't be able to account for it on my books. I can sell these tickets to this man over here, give you the refund on the meals, and take the rest home myself."

"If that's the case," I said, "I guess you'd better refund the tickets."

Instead of having only about two dollars, we now had about $450! The Lord gave us our personal version of the miracle of the loaves and fishes that early morning at the bustling Los Angeles International Airport. Never have we doubted Him since (though He's cut it close sometimes) when He said, "If you then, being evil know how to give good things to your children, how much more will your Father who is in heaven give what is good to those who ask Him?" (Matthew 7:11).

He wasn't just proposing a theological idea, or illustrating a sermon point, or giving the world another idea for some good gospel songs. What He said, He meant. And the only reason it hasn't been true in so many people's lives today—especially American Christians' lives—is that our self-sufficiency, self-security, and independence has excluded Him and eliminated a feeling of our need to trust Him. We have all the bases covered so well that God has nothing else to do but sit in the stands and cheer us on.

That first year we did little prayer groups, big concerts, revival meetings. We sang in high school assemblies, churches, Sunday schools, and coffeehouses. We did perhaps an average of ten concerts a week. Many times we gave up to six concerts a day! We didn't have to knock ourselves out like that but we loved every minute of it. We loved the traveling, the people, the ministry.

In the last five years we have not sent out one piece of promotional material. We have not made one call asking for an engagement. All our engagements have been results of invitations which were also results of our having been somewhere. We, or any organization, agency or man can not take the credit for the phenomenal growth of this ministry. It is God's thing.

10

Mainland Ministry

We spent our first three Christmases on the mainland with the Knopps in Virginia. I experienced my first snow that first Christmas and what fun we had throwing snowballs and going tobogganing. Diane wasn't feeling well a lot of the time though, and later we found out that we were expecting our first baby.

Our first tour following that Christmas was in Florida. On our flight down there, we were served a meal and of course Diane immediately began to feel ill. She said, "Lord, this is really ridiculous. If I am going to be sick on this trip, I would much rather be sick at home. So either I'm well on this trip, or I am going to go back to the Knopp's home or back to Hawaii and be sick there. There is no sense of being sick on the trip and not be any good to anybody. If you want me to go on this tour to Florida, then You make me so I am not sick."

She said that the nausea left immediately. She ate her meal and didn't have morning sickness again, even while she was carrying Christine, our second child.

DeAnna was expected to arrive in August, so we planned to go back to Hawaii in June and spend the entire summer in the islands.

I had written several letters to our friends and family in Hawaii asking them to find an apartment for us. We were going to live on our savings, if possible, or I would see if I could get a part-time job. We knew it would be difficult to find a job just for the summer, but we thought we could at least find a place to stay. We couldn't stay with our relatives because they didn't have enough room for all of us.

We got back to Hawaii in June and discovered that for some reason an apartment had not been secured. It slowly dawned on us that our families and friends in Hawaii didn't really know what we had been doing while we were on the mainland. We got little sympathy when we arrived home because their attitude was: You've been traipsing around the countryside, now it's about time you came home and settled down.

I could understand that; they had never been to any of our concerts. But it was still a blow to us.

We ended up in an apartment in a slummy part of Waikiki which was the only area that would rent to us on a month-to-month basis. The apartment was a sparsely furnished, hot, cockroach-infested fourth floor walk-up—for $250 a month!

It was downhill all the rest of the summer. Things got worse and worse. I couldn't get a job, no one wanted to listen to our sad story, and we didn't have a lot of concerts to give. It seemed that we had really missed it somewhere.

People didn't mind us coming to sing in their churches as we had before—for the offering or a few special numbers—but nobody was prepared for The Hawaiians in a concert! Their attitude was: You're our own family, and you don't take a love offering from your own family. And for us to say, "Instead of coming and singing a few songs, let us give a full concert," was presumptuous.

We didn't have much income, so we had to spend our savings. We went through everything. When we had been in Hawaii for about a month, our accompanist, who was from Hawaii and had joined us on the mainland, decided not to return with us at the end of the summer. This hit us like a lead balloon. It wasn't Randy's fault; it was just God's timing in the situation. The Lord was trying to get us back to the mainland. We had returned to Hawaii with the idea that if things went well, we would just stay. But after about a month and a half in the "Paradise of the Pacific," we were aching to leave.

A pastor friend of ours gave us a verse, Isaiah 30:15: "In quietness and confidence shall be your strength." We couldn't ask anybody to pray for us, because all of the people were praying that we would stay in Hawaii.

At about this time, the church we were attending had planned a Sunday morning summer musicale. The pastor had told us in a letter several months earlier that we should keep the last Sunday in August free. In Hawaii, you don't ask to sing, you wait until you are asked. We waited until the Saturday before that particular Sunday, and still no one had asked us to sing. We found out later that since we had done a concert at the church several weeks before, some people who were on for that morning said they weren't going to participate if we were going to sing—we would make them look bad.

I could understand their feelings. But nobody had told us anything because they thought, "We'll give Mark and Diane a break and let them rest." They didn't know that our morale was at a very low ebb.

We planned to get to church that morning five minutes after the service was to begin. But the only available seats were at the front of the sanctuary; we had to walk down in front of everyone. We were dying inside—what a humiliation. Soon the choir director sent a note down,

"Would you please sing in the choir this morning, we need a tenor."

In my mental and emotional state, it seemed to be a meager, last-minute effort to make us feel like we belonged. I sang, but we left before the service was over. "Hon," I said to Diane, "as soon as you have this baby, let's pack up and go to the mainland."

God was using all of this. We were scheduled the next weekend to be one of several groups who were to provide the music at a big luau sponsored by one of the large churches in Honolulu. We were also scheduled to minister at a Teen Challenge rally that night.

Randy, our former accompanist, is one of the most versatile pianists I have ever known. With him we were able to sing all kinds of styles—from old-fashioned Hawaiian to contemporary rock.

I didn't think we could present a good program without Randy playing for us. There wasn't any way we could fool the Hawaiian music buffs at the luau, and then go with my autoharp to sing, "Sweet, Sweet Spirit" to hippie kids at a Teen Challenge rally.

If only Randy could be here now, Randy could handle all of this. I just didn't think we could do without him. I was convinced we were going to make the biggest flops of our lives—and both on the same night!

One night I just couldn't stand it any longer. I went out into the living room of the apartment and wept. (I've done a lot of weeping in this book. Maybe it should be titled *The Wet Hawaiian.*) I said, "Lord, I just don't see how I'm going to do it. If this is forecasting things to come, how are we going to do any of those months of concerts we have lined up on the mainland? How are we going to do it without Randy? How am I going to play the piano and sing? I've never done that before."

To make a long story short, we went to the luau and

sang several Hawaiian songs as I played my autoharp, and the response was great. Then we went to the Teen Challenge rally. I can play the piano a bit, so I could have gotten by. But all they had was a big organ, and I didn't know how to play it.

I could do only slow songs, so we sang, "Take my reputation, take my nearest blood relation." I felt like the 200 kids were going to murder us, or fall asleep or get up and walk out. But for our last song, the third of three slow "sleepers," I felt led to sing, "Savior, Like a Shepherd Lead Us." That's super-slow.

I took my autoharp and said, "You know, this is an oldie, and it was taught to us by the missionaries. My grandmother taught me the Hawaiian translation. I would like to sing it now. Most of you are going to be really bored, but I want to sing it as a testimony to what God has done for me this last year.

"I never knew I had any real prejudices against white people until I went to the mainland and spent the entire year there. Everybody was so nice to us. I recalled how I used to deliver papers to all these fancy white *haoles* up on 'Snob Hill,' and they wouldn't even come out and say hi. I was just one of the local little urchins. I had to go to Hilo Union School because I wasn't in the class of the kids who went to Riverside Elementary.

"A lot of resentment came out. Here we were spending all our energy, our lives, entertaining these little old ladies in their white frocks in these huge fancy white churches when my own people would not accept the Lord. The Hawaiian people were completely turned off by Christianity because of the way these people were. My people were going to go to hell. These white people were all going to heaven and my people were going to burn. And I really had to come to the Lord about that.

"But I want to sing this song now because God has

brought you kids to Hawaii." (Most of the kids in that group were rejects from the mainland. They just came over and started living on Hawaii's beaches.)

"Most of you kids here are just here to use up all of our land, use up our air, use up our beaches, sit in our streets. I could be really resentful about you. God brought you here because He wants to speak to you and God took me to the mainland because He wanted to speak to me. I think if we listen to him we ought to get something real good."

So we sang the song, "Savior, Like a Shepherd Lead Us," and sat down. What we didn't know was that Ruby was in the audience.

11
Ruby

A girl friend of mine came over to the house where I was living with a family by the name of Becks and asked me if I would go to a rally with her.

"What kind of a rally?" I asked.

"A real neat Teen Challenge rally," she answered. "A lot of kids are there; it's a real blast."

I didn't want to go. I was on heroin and all kinds of other drugs and was sick. I told her, "No, I don't want to go. Just leave me alone. Please!"

But she wouldn't leave me alone; she kept bugging me, bugging me and bugging me. Finally, just to get her off my back, I said, "All right, I'll go!"

The rally was held in an Assembly of God church. It was different from anything I'd ever been to—drug addicts usually don't frequent churches. The people there were loving and friendly. There were a lot of young kids there, mostly hippie kids. They'd come to me and say, "Hi! We love you . . ." and all that. I didn't grow up in a family of love so I didn't know what love was. I simply couldn't understand it. All I could think was, *What do they want out of me? Why are they so friendly?* I went into the church after I had pushed all these people away from me and sat in the last pew, way at the back of the church. My girl friend wanted to go sit way up front; those great people were singing and she didn't want to miss anything. I stayed in the back.

Mark and Diane stood up and they shared. Diane was pregnant. Mark started talking about their travels to the mainland and how good it was to be back in Hawaii. He was talking about Jesus, and Jesus' aloha. During the whole time something was happening to me. I was responding to what he was saying. He said he was going to sing a song that his grandmother had taught him when he was young: "Jesu no ke kahu hipa"—"Savior Like a Shepherd Lead Us". When I was a kid, I used to sing that song in Hawaiian, but never knew the meaning of it. I had picked up the song coming out of church. I sang it when I'd wash the dishes; everything I did I sang that song.

The words really touched me. It did something to me. I didn't know what it was doing; all I know is that it was breaking down barriers. Walls that I had built up for years. Before I realized it, I was sitting there crying and I couldn't stop. I hadn't cried since I was nine years old. Through the whole service I kept crying.

Mark just went on and after he finished his song, he talked more about Jesus and how He could help you if you had all these hangups, if you would just bring them to Him. What really hit me was that he made it look like Jesus loved me, and no one else in this whole world did. I was searching for love; that's why I was into all these other things. The Becks took me home, but I couldn't stop crying. They finally called their pastor. He came to the house to pray. He said the only thing he could think of was that the Holy Spirit was working on me.

In the church that night, when Mark and Diane had asked us to take a step and ask the Lord to come into our lives, I had, but I hadn't told anybody. I had made that commitment in myself, praying, "Jesus, if You're real, like this man Mark talks about, like Diane talks about, come in my life and do something with me. Help me!" I was at the point where I didn't really care whether I lived or not. I really felt that God came in at that time. I went through the whole evening and they left me alone. I sobbed until finally I stopped.

Three days later I went to another meeting at Teen Challenge. A guy got up and gave his testimony, saying just about the same thing Mark had said. It was all about the love of Jesus, only he gave an invitation to come forward and make this public. He used the Scripture, "If you confess me before men, I will confess you before the Father." So I went forward. I ended up running down that aisle—it was like I couldn't get there in time.

I was still on drugs. I had run down the aisle, and when I got there, all I know is that I threw myself on the floor and I cried out to God saying, "God help me or let me die right now! If you can't help me I want to die!"

At that moment, for the first time in my life—it's hard to explain—Jesus came and put His arms around me. For the first time I felt that somebody loved me. I couldn't understand it, I couldn't feel it, or see it, but yet...there was just knowing in the peace that came over me. I lay there on the floor for a long time. the next thing I knew, people were around me, praying for me.

On my way home, all I could think of was God and getting another "fix." I could hardly wait to get out the needle I still wanted and needed to get my fix of heroin. I knew something had happened but I didn't fully realize what.

My hands were shaking but I knew in a minute everything would be okay—the fix always calmed me. I was ready to shoot up when the whole mess dropped out of my hand and went down the drain.

Pain and fear gripped me. I knew the pain of withdrawal. In minutes I would be climbing the walls with pain. Minutes went by and no pain. I waited and wondered, *What's happening?* The night was passing and still no withdrawal pains. Then I realized God was doing something with my life. "He is all I need, He is all I need," I cried. After ten years of heroin, I was free! He really loves me!

Then I saw Mark and Diane again. The Becks had invited them over to the house to have dinner with us. I got to meet them face to face and share what their testimony meant to me.

I left the Becks and went to Teen Challenge. Soon after this I went through their rehabilitation program. I worked on the staff of Teen Challenge and got involved in the choir. Off and on I saw Mark and Diane. When they were leaving the Islands for the mainland, we joked about my going along; of course we were just kidding. "Wouldn't it be neat if you could come along with us," Mark would say.

"Oh, yes," I said, "it'd be nice if I could just travel with you and take care of the baby." Soon they were gone and that was the end of them, I thought.

At Teen Challenge I was going through many things while I was working there. I felt I wanted a job—a steady job. My salary wasn't enough to keep up payments for my apartment. Sometimes I got only five dollars a month, and sometimes nothing at all. I enjoyed being there because it was a new life and that's what God wanted me to do. So I was looking for a job and yet it seemed every door was closed. I prayed and prayed, and everybody prayed with me, and all the doors stayed closed. I thought this whole Christianity thing is worse—it's worse being a Christian; as a non-Christian I hadn't had to worry about money. I had ways of getting it.

I was still having problems with drugs. Off and on I would drink and pop pills. My life seemed empty and yet I knew God had touched me. The other kids (I was doing everything they were doing) were reading the Bible, singing in the choir, and their lives seemed fuller than my life was. I couldn't understand.

Then Mark's letter came and asked me if I'd join them in Dallas, care for the children and travel with them. I couldn't believe it! Why would anybody like Mark and Diane, who were well-known singers and good Christian people, want me, a drug addict, taking care of their baby and traveling around with them? But everybody was saying, "Ruby, yes! It's the Lord!"

"All right," I said, "if it's really the Lord, I'll have to get a ticket by this weekend." I was sort of freaked. So I said, "Well, all right, Lord, if this is really You, then by this weekend, I'll get an airline ticket."

So we wrote Mark and Diane, and the Becks wrote them too. Friday came—nothing. Saturday came—still nothing. So I went to the office and said, "See, I told you. It wasn't the Lord. Who in their right mind would hire a drug addict to take care of their kid? There's nobody in this world as good as that."

"Ruby," they said, "we really feel it's the Lord!"

"Well, then, you're wrong; take the hint!" I said.

On Sunday I went to church. Teen Challenge was showing the movie, *The Cross and the Switchblade,* at a local theater, and I was in charge of the tickets. In the middle of the service I got up and left to go down to the theater. On the way I had to stop at the office to pick up the cash box. There was a special delivery letter for me from Mark and Diane, and in it was the money for the airline ticket. I couldn't believe it. I sat down and screamed and cried. I cried all the way to the theater.

At that point I realized that I didn't want to leave Hawaii to join Mark and Diane because I knew they were Spirit-filled. I thought, *Lord, I don't want to join them! I don't even have the Holy Spirit in my life.* Of course I wasn't really seeking the filling of the Holy Spirit because I thought it was of the devil. So that night I went to church and prayed, "Lord, if being filled with the Holy Spirit is really of You, then I want it! Before I leave I want it!"

Later the pastor saw me and said, "Ruby, this is your night."

I didn't know what he was talking about. It so happened that he was talking about the baptism of the Holy Spirit, and that night I truly got filled with the Holy Spirit. What peace was mine; it flooded my being.

I caught the plane the next day and joined Mark and Diane in Dallas. I've been with them ever since. We've had our ups and downs because of my insecurities, but the Lord has really blessed us. I'd never known what it's like to live in a family, but I felt that with God putting me with Mark and Diane, He had given me a family. I belonged to someone.

Then we moved to Olathe—we moved in one day and the next day Mark and Diane left—and I found myself alone most of the time with the baby and Fred. Fred was in school and he had his own things to do. I didn't know anyone; I was afraid of people too, especially white people. I had a lot of resentment toward them because of my upbringing. So I really didn't want to get to know a lot of people there.

I was left alone and because of that I ended up going back into drugs, only I never told Mark and Diane. For two years we had traveled around together, and I hadn't taken drugs at all and there was no desire for them.

Then when we moved to Olathe, all of a sudden there was a need to belong again and I got very upset with God. "All right, God, You know I have tried," I said. I just really had it out with the Lord and I found myself fighting two spirits. I had some pills in my hand and was going to take them—the baby was asleep and Fred was gone. But there was a part of me saying, "No, you don't need that really. You don't really need that anymore."

Then I cried out to God, "Why? You gave Mark and Diane to me, and now You have taken everything away from me. Why?"

That night God showed me He didn't want me holding on to Mark and Diane, but to Him. I was putting my trust in Mark and Diane. "It's not them I want you to trust," God said. "I want you to trust Me and only Me. I am the One who has brought you this far. I am the One who has taken you out of the gutter and your loneliness and brought you here. You are not alone, but you don't look to Me—you look to Mark and Diane so that when they are gone, you are alone."

Then He brought me back to the night I first came to Him and how I had laid there on the floor and cried—the feeling I had as He touched me. Then I realized that I was holding on to Mark and Diane and putting them on a pedestal, and not really looking to the Lord. That was the last battle with drugs.

Since then I have learned, through a lot of struggle, to put all my trust in the Lord. I feel I have come a long way. I really enjoy having so many people in all the time; I feel there is really a ministry here with Mark and Diane. I just love them like my own family.

12
The Beginning of Something Big

During Christmas vacation 1970, we announced to all our friends, especially those on the eastern seaboard, that we were going to have a New Year's celebration. New Year is a big deal in Hawaii and we were disappointed that it wasn't much of anything on the mainland. We told them the celebration would last at least three days.

A couple of kids we had met the year before, Chad and Jay, came all the way from Florida with about seven of their friends to celebrate with us. Fran, who lived in Fort Lauderdale, was one of those friends.

One Sunday morning about two months later, we were singing at the First Baptist Church of Fort Lauderdale and Fran was there with her boyfriend and his parents. Her boyfriend's father was Walter Smyth who was with Billy Graham's international ministries. We were so pleased to meet them that we gave Walter and his family our albums. Later he wrote and asked if we would send some records to Cliff Barrows, which we did. We soon got a thank you from Cliff and we thought that was the end of that.

By this time Diane was pregnant with our second

child. It was funny at times, going back to some of the same places we had visited only the year before when Diane was expecting our DeAnna. She looked just the same, and people asked, "Haven't you had that baby yet?"

Diane insisted on singing in the concerts together with me until the week before the baby was due and a week after the baby had arrived.

Diane had had a very difficult birth with DeAnna; she was in labor for twenty-four hours. Of course I was there with her like a brave husband. I thought it would take a couple of hours at the most, so I took my autoharp, thinking I would sing for her to help ease her mind.

But she went on and on; it got worse and worse. For hours late into the night, every time she had a pain I would sing at the top of my lungs. That maternity ward will never be the same again. It was the first and last time they ever had anybody come into the labor room with an autoharp.

Diane finally had to have a Caesarean delivery. So now that she was expecting Christine, we could plan our schedule so we could give concerts up to the week of the baby's birth. Diane insisted on not staying home.

We planned Christine's birth so I would be able to catch a plane to Kansas City. She was born at 7:00, I saw her at 7:30, rushed to the airport and boarded the plane at 9:00 to fly to Kansas City for a series of concerts over the weekend.

After Christine was born we realized that we could no longer travel around in the same way. We would stay in one place for maybe a month and work out of that area until someone else invited us to their city. We were like wandering minstrels. Our residence was a post office box in Cleveland, Tennessee!

By this time Ruby had been with us for about eight

months. The Tyler Street Methodist Church, which had been our first stop when we came back to the mainland, invited us to Dallas. They had an empty parsonage which was up for sale, but we would be able to stay in it until it was sold. We moved all of our things to Dallas and spent four great months there. During this time we bought our first car and started driving from place to place.

We went back to Virginia to spend Christmas with the Knopps that year. We were driving back to Dallas and decided to stop in Cleveland for about fifteen minutes to get the mail.

In the short time we were in the post office someone from the church in Dallas called to say, "We're so glad we got you there. The parsonage was sold yesterday and the people want to move in tomorrow. We've already packed up all your things and we are storing them in the church. If you don't have any other place to go, come on back and we'll put you up in homes until we can find another place."

We had already been considering several states where we could settle. Since we were heading west, we called a friend in Kansas City and asked if he could help us find a place to stay there.

We immediately detoured to Kansas City and the next day began looking for a mobile home and a place to park it. We wanted a mobile home because we didn't have many personal belongings or furniture. The best mobile home park we saw was in Olathe, Kansas, about fifteen miles from Kansas City. We were ready to contract for a mobile home through a dealer who told us that it would take six to ten weeks to get it. There were many changes we had to make in the existing mobile home floor plans that he showed us; it had to accommodate Diane and me, Fred, Ruby, and the girls. What we really needed was a mobile home that was three stories tall!

We went to the park owner to sign up for a lot. He took us around to look at the different lots, and I saw the one I wanted. But a mobile home was already parked there.

"Have you looked at any of the mobile homes we have here?" he asked me.

"No, we haven't," I said.

"Would you like to come over and see ours?" he asked.

I told him we had already decided to purchase another mobile home. But then he took us right to the home that was on the lot I wanted. It was one of the models they had for sale; it was exactly what we were looking for. Everything we had—from the toilet covers to the salt and pepper shakers—matched its red and black Spanish decor. Everything was perfectly color-coordinated except Ruby's room—what she had collected was blue, so we teased her that she was out of the will of God.

Olathe has proven to be a convenient and central home; it's about as central as you can get in the United States.

Although we have now long since moved out of that mobile home, God used that year and a half we spent there to teach us more choice lessons about His kind of Forever Aloha.

Soon after we moved in, we found that all was not perfect about the home. The shower didn't work right; the doors stuck; Ruby's bathroom leaked constantly.

It occurred to me after the umpteenth time the repair man had come to fix the shower, that we were spending a lot of time, energy, and money fixing the house up. We had added shelves and hooks and had planted flowers in the yard. I knew this must be home.

During the years we have been on the road, we have had the privilege of staying in hundreds of homes and our hosts have always been cordial, hospitable and accommodating. They've all tried to make us feel at home. But not one of them, I think, would have wanted us to pound nails in the wall, dig up the yard to improve what was their home. We now had our home, and we felt free to do as we wished to make it what we wanted it to be.

Paul said in First Corinthians 6:19 that our bodies are the temples of the Holy Spirit. In the third chapter of Ephesians, the Living Bible paraphrases verse seventeen this way: "I pray that Christ will be more and more at home in your hearts, living within you as you trust in Him . . . ."

It occured to me that much of the time I was playing "host" to the Lord, asking Him to "make Himself at home" when all the time He wanted to own the house of my life. He wanted to make renovations and to fix whatever needed to be fixed, as he pleased.

If He is really to be "more and more at home" in our hearts, He must be free to pound nails where He wishes and to move entire walls (and don't we all have walls that need to be moved) if he wants to.

We weren't in our mobile home more than a couple of weeks when all these Toms, Dicks and Alices began to drop by again. We had told the Lord a long time ago, in our apartment in Hawaii, not to send anybody to us He didn't want us to have. Some kids would stop by; others would stay overnight.

Soon Ruby called, while we were on tour, to say that a kid had stopped by with his wife—they were hitchhiking across the nation. Ruby wanted to know whether or not we should allow them to stay with us. I had met the guy in North Carolina and he had said he was going to start hitchhiking across the country. I had said, "If you come to Kansas City, stop by. We'll try to give you a place to stay." I didn't know he was married.

Ruby had opened the door and the Lord told her that they weren't married—she sent them over to the neighbors to stay!

To make a long story short, when we got back from tour I talked to him and found out that they really weren't married. I told them that they couldn't carry on like this and that one of them would have to go. So the boy left. The girl was a woman in her mid-thirties and Ruby felt a responsibility to minister to her, so she stayed. The day after the guy left, Diane went to her jewelry box and found that her jade earrings and her opal ring were gone. She had worn the ring only once—I had given it to her for our fifth wedding anniversary.

"Well, Lord, that's it," I said. "I'm not going to have any more of these tramps coming into the house!"

The Lord spoke to me, "Mark, how are you going to tell which ones are tramps and which ones aren't? Are you going to have them fill out a form in the yard before you let them sit in your living room? Are you going to let them stay overnight? Who will you let only into the living room and not into the bedrooms?"

We had to make a renewed commitment of faith in the Lord, that He was and is Lord and He would take care of us. We had to trust that He would not bring anybody to the house He didn't want there. It was the law of love again: When you love, you entrust everything you are and have to the one you love.

It is as the hymn says, "Love so amazing, so divine, demands my soul, my life, my all." That means your jade earrings, opals, diamonds, house, furniture, kids, everything. This means then that if it is all God's, God can do anything He wants with it. If He wants to share it with the Toms, Dicks and Alices who come, that is His business and it's not really mine to lose. And that counts even when the loss is my own fault.

That's kind of hard for Americans to catch on to. It's kind of hard for anybody, but especially for Americans who spend their lives attaining things and positions and then trying to maintain what they've attained.

Most of us realize that involvement—real involvement—is a threat to ourselves. How many times we have questioned our own involvement with people. Involvements that have sometimes ended in disappointment and pain. It would be so much easier for us to just sing and talk about love and loving in our concerts, and then go home, close the doors and say, "Well, that's that. We've done our job." But God has chosen to have us live out every day the kind of love we sing about.

For self-preservation purposes, most people have learned to love with limits. We love until we are betrayed, until it becomes an inconvenience, or until loving becomes too much of a risk. God doesn't love that way and we are learning more and more the price of His kind of love.

We met Michael one night backstage after a Youth For Christ rally in Kansas City. We learned during our short conversation that he was one of the thousands of youngsters in America who are the relics of people who loved and lost. Michael had been living in foster homes since he was a child and at the time we met him, he had been living for two and a half years at a halfway house for boys waiting to be placed in foster homes.

Before long, sixteen-year-old Michael became a part of our family. (What should we have said to him, "Run along and be a good boy. We'll drop you a line sometime"?) He was a dear young man who yearned for people who would really love him, no matter what.

We became his family and he became our son. We planned to adopt him when he became eighteen and was free of the state's jurisdiction. On his seventeenth birthday we gave him a ring inscribed with his Hawaiian name: Ka-mea-aloha-emauloa-ahemolele (He who has begun that good work within you will continue it until He brings you to complete perfection in eternity, Philippians 1:16 paraphrased).

Time and again we wondered if our love was being well-invested. The normal hassles of a seventeen-year-old were magnified by his lack of good early foundational training and our being away from home so much. We were told that there was nowhere he could go if he left—he would be sent to the boy's reformatory.

We hung on and watched as Michael slowly but surely responded to our love.

Then, nine months after he had come to live with us, Michael left. Just up and left, because according to him, he couldn't take the demands, we didn't really love him, and he could take care of himself. Our initial reaction was one of anger, frustration and chagrin.

While flying to California the next week, in my heaviness of heart, I said, "Lord, I guess this is what the story of the prodigal son was all about."

To my surprise, the Lord spoke to my spirit and said, "No, Mark."

"Well, what is it then?"

The Lord said, "The story of the prodigal son is the story of My love for you. Michael's story is the story of your love for Me. The prodigal son knew who his father was and he knew that any time he wanted to he could go back home. Michael was never sure that you were really his parents. So he never learned that you loved him and that he could trust you, believe you and love you. And you and so many other Christians are like Michael. Because you're not really sure who your Father is, you are always wavering in your trust and your love for Me."

Michael has not returned to us. But we told him (against our human judgment) that because of our commitment of love to the Lord, our commitment of love to him would go on forever and that he would always find our hearts, our lives, our home open to him.

Fred entered Olathe High School as a junior, and was elected student body president. This was an honor for all of us—especially considering from whence Fred had come.

One day he came home with a report card that had put him on the honor roll for the first time in his life. When he first came to us, he was getting straight F's in school and academics had never been his strong point. After we all rejoiced together, he confided to me that when the report cards were handed out in class and he saw what he had, he immediately wanted to tell his friends—until their "so what" response reminded him that being on the honor roll was no big deal for them. They had been on the roll for years!

When we could, we went to his school's meetings. It was traumatic to go to those meetings and have people ask what school we were from—they thought we were kids from another school crashing the party. When Fred introduced us to his teacher and said, "These are my parents," the teacher would raise his eyebrow and give us a strange look because we were so young.

After one of those occasions, I talked to Fred about it. "Fred, don't you think you should make a special explanation to your teachers or to anybody you introduce us to, that we are your adopted parents?"

Fred said, "No."

"Why?"

"Because you are my mother and father and that's tough if they don't understand."

"Come on, Fred," I said. "We don't have the wrinkles

and pot-bellies that other people who have children your age do, you know. We don't look old enough to be parents of a seventeen-year-old. (At that time I was twenty-seven.) What do you really see me as? Do you really see me as your father?"

He put his head down and thought for a long time. Then he looked up with big tears in his eyes—this big football hero and karate expert—and said, "Dad, it is just like you are my very best friend."

That really touched me. I used to wish that I could tell my father that he was my best friend. But my father was from another generation and they weren't like that. For Fred to tell me that I was his best friend was like a lot of pigeons coming home to finally find their resting place. It was beautiful.

Soon after that I re-discovered Romans five, starting with the sixth verse. It now had special meaning: *When we were his enemies, we were brought to God by the death of His Son, what blessings He must have for us now that we are His friends and He is living within us. Now we rejoice in our wonderful new relationship with God—all because of what our Lord Jesus Christ has done in dying for our sins—making us friends of God* (Living Bible).

The whole thing about my wanting a friend when I was a kid came alive again. The reason we have such a need for fellowship, for true friendship, is because we were made in God's image. God wants us for His friends. In Hawaii, a real friend is someone you can "talk story" with. There are so many things He wants to share in confidence with us. He's looking for people who will allow them to walk and talk and laugh and share secrets together. God is looking for friends.

13
On Our Way

During the summer of 1972, we spent almost two months on the east coast. When we returned home, our coordinator said, "I have a weekend in November that just doesn't seem to be shaping up at all. The entire weekend was canceled once and I set it up again. It was canceled all over again—this is highly unusual."

(We have canceled very few engagements during our ministry. The main reasons for these cancellations have been conflicts in dates or some disagreement with our doctrinal stand—which I think is ridiculous in the life of the Spirit and in the family of God.)

I said, "Well, will we have any difficulty filling it?"

"Oh, no," he said, "Lots of places I can send you to."

"Why don't we just wait and see what the Lord has, because He must have something special for that weekend. Maybe He just wants us to stay home." At this time we were averaging about forty concerts a month.

The next day we got a letter from Cliff Barrows who invited us to the Billy Graham Crusade in St. Louis in November and asked for the weekend which had been canceled twice. We were excited! Working with the Billy Graham team has been a tremendous experience.

Since that weekend we have been invited to the Billy Graham Phoenix Crusade, the Congress on World Evangelization in Switzerland, the Hollywood Bowl Crusade and the Norfolk Crusade in 1974.

Cliff Barrows had called me about a month after the St. Louis Crusade. He said, "Mark, would you consider going with us to Lausanne, Switzerland?"

And without thinking, I reacted, "Would we? Diane and I just love cheese fondue."

There was a long silence and I realized I hadn't said the right thing. "That didn't sound very spiritual, did it?" I said and we both broke into howls of laughter.

But Diane and I didn't get to Switzerland because we both came down with viral infections.

I had had three ambitons as a kid in college. One was to sing on the stage of the Metropolitan Opera; another was to go to Switzerland; the third was that if I ever made an album, I wanted to have it played by Bill Pearce on his "Night Watch" (now Night Sounds") program.

After we were invited to Lausanne, all these things came back to me.

In February, 1974, we had just finished a concert in Fargo, North Dakota, and I was telling our host and hostess about these childhood dreams—I don't know how we got onto the subject. They turned on the car radio and there was Bill Pearce's "Night Sounds". "There is a very special couple I want you to listen to," Bill said. He started to play "No Name on Earth Has Meant So Much To Me", a song which Diane and I had put on our latest album. Cold chills ran up and down my spine.

I turned to Diane and said, "Well, I guess that after July I can just lay down and die." We were supposed to be in Switzerland that month, but we didn't make it. So I guess I can live a little while longer.

In our kind of business, the stewardship of time, energy, and money is so important. Let me share a bit of my own philosophy about these things and how God has helped us to maintain what a lot of people think is a unique stand on finances and sales.

First of all, the sales of our records and tapes. For the first three years of our concertizing, I rarely talked about the records we had available. I usually asked the host pastor to announce it for us, and most of the time this resulted in people not taking our albums very seriously.

But many people told us, "Mark and Diane, you really should announce those albums and get them into people's hands because they are such a blessing." We would answer, "We just don't want to be identified with the kind of zoo that sometimes goes on in gospel concerts when records are being promoted."

One day while we were traveling across the Arizona deserts, the Lord seemed to speak to me. "Mark," He said, "why don't you announce those albums?"

I gave Him our usual answer.

"Well, if you don't like to sell things in church, why don't you give them away?"

I said, "Oh, Lord, that can't be You. Get thee behind me, Satan!"

But it was the Lord and He was trying to stimulate me into thinking about some new concepts.

So what do we do with our records? We now tell people that albums are available, encouraging those who can't afford an album to come to the record table and let us give them one. We don't think anyone should miss the blessing because they don't have money.

We also tell people that if they try to get a free album by saying they can't afford it when they really can, they will break out in a Hawaiian rash every time they listen to the record!

When we first started out, we were in Cleveland, Tennessee, with Norvel Hayes. We sang at a church with about thirteen people attending, and the offering was only about seven dollars. Norvel said apologetically, "Well, Mark, sometimes that's the way it goes."

I didn't want him to feel badly, but I didn't know what to say. I opened my mouth to reply, and I believe my response was from the Lord. I said, "Norvel, if we were in this thing for the money we would have taken those entertainment jobs in Hawaii. There are a lot of ways that musicians can make money if they want to. But if we are going to do this thing at all, we are going to do it for the Lord. Everything we get will come from Him. So whether it is seven dollars or seven thousand, it doesn't make any difference to Him, our needs will be supplied."

Since then we have been quite firm about our preference for love offerings. We believe that each individual should be allowed to respond in a financial way as he feels directed. The offerings should be a response of love to God, not a show of appreciation to The Hawaiians or a show of support for our ministry. If people respond to Him, He will bless us and provide all our needs.

We don't have a minimum amount for love offerings. We will gladly receive anything from a penny on up because the Lord told us a long time ago that our minimum will also be our maximum.

As our ministry has grown, we have been in many situations, at banquets and in churches on set budgets, where love offerings are not possible. In these we ask for a fee.

When we go by love offerings, we go by faith. But if we are going to ask for a fee, we are going by sight, and being very near-sighted, we feel we should ask for as much as we can! We learned that a large fee will completely take care of all our needs without any faith involved. But how much more of a joy to be able to place all our finances in His hand.

14
Aloha . . . the Forever Kind

The week after Fred came to stay with us he went with a group of young people to a Bible study. There they asked everyone to turn to a favorite Scripture and expound on it.

He didn't have any Scripture; he didn't know any Bible verses. So he just opened up his brand new Bible that I had given him for his birthday; it fell open to Psalm 27. He then read it to the group, "The Lord is my light and my salvation . . . though my mother and father forsake me, yet the Lord will take me up."

That has been his theme chapter ever since then because it fits him so perfectly.

When we first started touring, one of the things that bothered me was that I didn't think I had any profound things to say. I've never considered myself to be a deep thinker or a deeply spiritual person or a learned student of the Bible. All that we ever share with people even today is what the Lord has worked out of and in our lives.

It was only through retrospect after our first year of ministry that we realized that the Lord had called us to a ministry of love. That He wanted us to stimulate His people to the kind of healing, reconciling, forgiving, sacrificial, creative Love that He is.

Time and again He's had to take us through the wringer to renew our warped concepts and ideas. We are becoming increasingly aware that there's an awful lot that we call Christian or "love" that has little to do with God or love.

It has been said that love is not love unless it is expressed. It is not just something you feel, but something you do. It's basically a verb, action.

That's why God had to reveal Himself in the way He did. Jesus was God with our bodies, our hassles, our feelings. He became the God who was touchable, approachable, and empathetic, the loving, feeling God whose "heart is touched with our grief."

It is a mistake to assume that the sovereign God Who is perfect does not crave love in return. True love—agape love—will keep on loving even though that love is never reciprocated. But that says nothing of the tremendous, continuous pain and hurt that is experienced when that love is rejected.

So many of us think of God as some kind of love machine which constantly throws out a universal aloha. It is not so much that God needs our love, but that God's nature of Love is the very reason He has the capacity to be loved so much.

As long as we do not love Him as He wants to be loved, He experiences hurt, loneliness and sadness. That is why He goes out of His way for us. Otherwise He would have dropped us a long time ago. We are very valuable to Him. Ephesians 1:18 says, ". . . I want you to realize that God has been made rich because we who are Christ's have been given to him!" (Living Bible).

When I first read that about three years ago, I nearly

fell on my nose. My initial thinking was, of course, that anyone who has committed themselves to the Lord has given all of himself to God. I could see why the Lord would be rich. Then it occurred to me that, in my own case, I had committed myself to the Lord so I was now "singing for the Lord." And the Lord impressed on my spirit that His most monotone and tone deaf angels had ten thousand better voices than I had. That it wasn't my singing that turned Him on, because His angels could sing a lot better.

I thought, *Well, surely it must be because of all of the sweat, blood and tears that all the saints have spent on the field of service.* I taught Sunday school, I directed the choir, witnessed to my friends, cleaned the toilets downstairs—all the work that conscientious Christians do. Then I read in the Gospels of how turned off Jesus was with the leaders of the Church of His day. He was not impressed with their service, their sacrifice, their orthodoxy, and their defense of the church.

Then I thought, *Well, of course, all the sacrificial giving that has gone on.* But I remembered that in Heaven are streets of gold so that couldn't be what makes God rich.

The fact is that He has enough angels to do all the things in the world that need to get done except that He has chosen *people* to do His greatest work in the universe, to bring the universe back together in harmony. The key for that harmony, the key to that song, is called *love.* There is no harmony unless there is love, the forever kind.

He has chosen us—people who are basically selfish and unloving—to bring everything back to the basis of love which is God Himself. What makes us valuable to God is that, when knowing how self-centered we are, knowing how ratty we are and inconsistent and undependable we are, we go to Him and say, "Lord, because I love You, all that I am and have are yours." We give ourselves to Him as love-presents. That makes God rich because we are the only creations in the universe that can love Him like that. Gold streets, angels, beautiful sunsets, even roses with the sparkle of dew cannot love God that way. We are the only ones who can voluntarily fill His heart with love.

That's how much we, His love-creations, mean to the God of love. And I am the only one in His entire universe, in all of His eternity, who can love Him like *I* can. That's why He will, at the drop of a hat, leave the ninety-nine in the fold and go out of His way for the one sheep that is lost. That sheep is one of a kind and nothing and no one can take its place.

If love is not love unless it is expressed, it is also true that love means nothing to the loved person until he responds to love. And then that love is meaningful only to the degree of the response. So although God expressed His love in the ultimate way by giving His Son to die in our places, His love means very little to people until they as individuals respond to that love. And because love is a deep and personal thing, that response must be a deep and personal one.

For this reason, our ministry has never been a "spectacular" one as far as numbers of converts and manifestations of the Spirit are concerned.

There was a time when I felt that we were somehow less than "spiritual" because our manner of encouraging people to respond personally to God's Aloha, at whatever level they could best respond, often resulted in commitments that were made quietly without much outward show.

Somehow when people are asked to respond to God on a deep love level, that response comes more slowly than it would if it came out of a fear of punishment, a sense of obligation, or to fulfill tradition. We encourage the people to count the cost and to respond personally in love to the Lord in a way that He will be more and more free to express His love through them to their world no matter what the cost.

That's a difficult commitment because most of us don't want to be hurt; we have too much to protect. We don't want to lose our self-identity in His all encompassing, cross-carrying Aloha.

But we are finding that there are thousands of people who want to make that commitment. Good Christian people who down deep realize that the reason so many people in the world are not Christians is not because they've rejected Christ. They've not even had Him presented in an honest, truthful, loving way. Most non-Christians have either never had the opportunity to make an intelligent choice (decision) or they (and this is true I think for most non-Christian Americans) have simply rejected the Christianity they *see!*

We have committed ourselves to a Christ who has been boxed up in our traditions, our doctrines, our methods, and our programs. For hundreds of years we have committed ourselves to "truth" (our interpretation of God's Word) and as a result have sacrificed the unity of the Body, knit together in *love,* on the altar of our doctrinal stances. We saw it in the Reformation. We see it between denominations. We see it between the "tonguers" and the "non-tonguers."

Jesus, in His prayer to the Father for all of us just before He went to the cross, prayed, "that they may be one; even as We are one; I in them and Thou in Me, that they may be perfected in unity, that the world may know that Thou didst send me . . . ." (John 17:22,23). The majority of our world still does not know that Jesus was truly the Son of God because His followers have not been one.

Someone said, "God has been known as the God of Love. Have His people been known as the people of love?" They have not. But there is a stirring in the land, a wind in the trees, a coming together of God's people today that is surpassing any spiritual awakening in the history of the world.

God is calling together a people who will fulfill the first commandment to love Him with everything they are and have. People are responding to Him in such a way that He is flowing His healing, reconciling, sacrificial love through them to His Church and to the world.

We are beginning to find an exhilaration in our worship so that we are freer to be openly expressive where we were once passive and reserved. On the other hand, our more overt brothers are discovering the strength that comes from quiet confidence.

Because of this flowing of God's Forever Aloha we are being freed from our fear of emotion, (Have you ever seen an unemotional love affair? But we are also experiencing a renewing, a strengthening of our minds. We're not afraid of intellectual, analytical discussions when based and motivated by this kind of Love.

We are relating to God as our Heavenly Father who is our best Friend! He is no more just a fire escape or a last resort or a Deity who reigns in majesty on High. He is a Person—a personal Person!

As a result, we are less often viewing people as things. Evangelists are not just traveling spiritual vendors. Gospel musicians are not just promotional objects for a fund-raising concert. Pastors and pastors' wives are not just guardians of the faith.

We are seeing all of God's people as individual persons with individual and very real needs. (How many preachers can get up before their congregations and say, "I'm a man of deep needs just like you. I need help. Pray for me"?)

As we learn to respond in love to the Lord and to minister to Him, He is teaching us to love and minister to each other, no matter who we are and who the other person is. We are learning to forgive and bless where we once used to reject and criticize.

And as God's kind of Forever Aloha permeates our lives we are discovering that in Him all things and all loves find completeness and fulfillment. There is no more need for the Christian agape (Godly), phileo (brotherly), and eros (sexual) categories of love.

The life inebriated by God's Forever Aloha will find a wholeness in all the other love areas of our lives. Relationships between husband and wife (including their sex life) will flow with God's kind of beauty and togetherness. The hearts of the children will be turned back to their parents. Our friendships will take on a deep permanence.

Loving God and fulfilling Him first will affect our sense of values and priorities. We will not make value judgments simply on the basis of economics or position or personal gain. Our investment of time, energy and money will be affected. Even our actions, reactions and our whole sense of decorum.

As we give ourselves to Him, He will share us as love-gifts to His world. To our spouses, our sweethearts, our friends, our families, our associates, our employers and employees our churches, our schools, our clubs, our government, we become His instruments of peace and happiness and redemption. So when someone responds negatively to your goodness, they are not really responding to you (the gift) but to God (the Giver). What a wonderful, divine way to pass the buck!

But this kind of loving in our kind of world will often invite pain and disappointment. It was exactly this kind of all-committing love that sent Jesus to the cross. But it is only this kind of dying that results in resurrection. And it is only that death motivated by His love (as opposed to the church's music program, or my interpretation of I Corinthians 14, or the preservation and propagation of my denominational doctrines) that will result in being "raised with Him."

One of these days there will be no need of churches or preachers or gospel musicians like The Hawaiians. The controversies of tongues and baby baptism and the characteristics of true holiness will be resolved. The object of our faith and hope will have been fulfilled. In that day, only those deeds motivated by God's Forever Aloha will remain. Only those energies, those monies and that time invested into His Forever Aloha will earn return and rewards.

In that day, He will draw from the north, the south, the east, and the west His Forever Aloha Family and we will live and love and sing and dance and laugh and work and play in the vast unlimited regions of the Kingdom of Aloha with the King of Aloha . . . Forever!